T0379864

The Selfish Year

The Selfish Year

The Selfish Year

The Power of Putting Yourself First

Valerie Jones

JB JOSSEY-BASS™
A Wiley Brand

Copyright © 2025 by Valerie Jones. All rights reserved.

Published by John Wiley & Sons, Inc., Hoboken, New Jersey.
Published simultaneously in Canada.

No part of this publication may be reproduced, stored in a retrieval system, or transmitted in any form or by any means, electronic, mechanical, photocopying, recording, scanning, or otherwise, except as permitted under Section 107 or 108 of the 1976 United States Copyright Act, without either the prior written permission of the Publisher, or authorization through payment of the appropriate per-copy fee to the Copyright Clearance Center, Inc., 222 Rosewood Drive, Danvers, MA 01923, (978) 750-8400, fax (978) 750-4470, or on the web at www.copyright.com. Requests to the Publisher for permission should be addressed to the Permissions Department, John Wiley & Sons, Inc., 111 River Street, Hoboken, NJ 07030, (201) 748-6011, fax (201) 748-6008, or online at http://www.wiley.com/go/permission.

The manufacturer's authorized representative according to the EU General Product Safety Regulation is Wiley-VCH GmbH, Boschstr. 12, 69469 Weinheim, Germany, e-mail: Product_Safety@wiley.com.

Trademarks: Wiley and the Wiley logo are trademarks or registered trademarks of John Wiley & Sons, Inc. and/or its affiliates in the United States and other countries and may not be used without written permission. All other trademarks are the property of their respective owners. John Wiley & Sons, Inc. is not associated with any product or vendor mentioned in this book.

Limit of Liability/Disclaimer of Warranty: While the publisher and author have used their best efforts in preparing this book, they make no representations or warranties with respect to the accuracy or completeness of the contents of this book and specifically disclaim any implied warranties of merchantability or fitness for a particular purpose. No warranty may be created or extended by sales representatives or written sales materials. The advice and strategies contained herein may not be suitable for your situation. You should consult with a professional where appropriate. Further, readers should be aware that websites listed in this work may have changed or disappeared between when this work was written and when it is read. Neither the publisher nor authors shall be liable for any loss of profit or any other commercial damages, including but not limited to special, incidental, consequential, or other damages.

For general information on our other products and services or for technical support, please contact our Customer Care Department within the United States at (800) 762-2974, outside the United States at (317) 572-3993 or fax (317) 572-4002.

Wiley also publishes its books in a variety of electronic formats. Some content that appears in print may not be available in electronic formats. For more information about Wiley products, visit our web site at www.wiley.com.

Library of Congress Cataloging-in-Publication Data:

ISBN 9781394342716 (Hardback)
ISBN 9781394342723 (ePub)
ISBN 9781394342730 (ePDF)

Cover Design: Wiley
Cover Images: © Yanka/stock.adobe.com, © cagkansayin/Getty Images
Author Photo: © Monika Sosnowska

SKY10121709_071125

For every woman who dares to dream for more.

self•ish /ˈselfiSH/

adjective

1. The radical act of honoring your truth, needs, and desires without guilt or apology.

2. Choosing self-trust over people-pleasing, even when it's uncomfortable.

3. A sacred rebellion against martyrdom, self-abandonment, and invisibility.

4. The foundation for generous, joyful, sustainable giving – born from overflow, not obligation.

Example: She stopped explaining, pleasing, and shrinking. Some called it coming home.

Contents

Prologue		ix
Introduction		xv
Chapter 1:	The Sofa of Truth	1
Chapter 2:	Rock Bottom	23
Chapter 3:	Running Back to Myself	43
Chapter 4:	Doorways	65
Chapter 5:	Wandering	83
Chapter 6:	The Cave	113
Chapter 7:	Haunted by the Past	133
Chapter 8:	No Risk, No Magic	159
Chapter 9:	Bird Set Free	185
Epilogue		203
Resources		209
Acknowledgments		211
About the Author		213

Prologue

I have a story to tell you.

It's a story that goes as far back as the roots of my family tree. Women have been telling it for generations, and it might be yours, too.

The story goes like this.

Once upon a time, there was a little girl. Let's call her *First Girl*. She loved to play, skip, and sing. She knew she was special, and she loved staring in the mirror at those eyes looking back at her. She didn't even consider that there was anything wrong with her. She might be eight, or four, or even younger, but she was happy, free, and full of love and light. She knew what she wanted and asked for it with certainty that it was hers for the taking. She greeted those around her with a wide smile and shining eyes.

She played with abandon and imagination. She loved with a big open heart, laughed with her belly, and lived with trust and openness.

Then something happened that changed her. It didn't happen in an instant, but rather a string of moments that, over time, transformed that happy, free little girl into someone very different. Let's call her *Hurt Girl*.

Hurt Girl didn't like looking in the mirror anymore. She became quiet and withdrawn. Instead of greeting everyone with a smile, she began hiding behind her mother's legs and looking down. Instead of asking for what she wanted and needed, she grew silent. She started looking at her body and finding things wrong with it. She began to escape into books, music, sports, or academics to find approval instead of simply because she loved it. She dressed for others instead of for herself. She began comparing herself to her friends and to other girls she saw at school or in magazines and online. She began to disconnect from the part of her that was love and began listening to a growing voice inside that told her to be afraid. The more she listened to that voice, the more she believed it when it told her she wasn't enough. She started believing that everyone else's happiness mattered more than her own.

Hurt Girl learned that abandoning herself was how to get love and approval, so she became really good at it. She shape-shifted to be who others needed her to be: quiet, good, polite, modest, smart, pretty, athletic, funny, helpful. Fitting in felt safe, and Hurt Girl was all about staying safe. She learned how to play by the rules, keep out of trouble, and survive. First Girl didn't fit in this new world. Her loud laugh, silly ways, and loud opinions weren't welcome.

It wasn't safe for First Girl anymore, so Hurt Girl stepped up. She knew what needed to be done. Eventually, it felt normal to play these roles, and First Girl, locked away and silenced, disappeared.

Now that little girl has grown up into a Woman, at least on the outside. On the inside, Hurt Girl still lives there and keeps making sure that the Woman does all the right things so she will be safe. First Girl is still locked away, shoved in a closet, with duct tape over her mouth. This agreement has been going on for decades now, and it's a slick operation. It's second nature. It's normal.

The only problem is, the Woman doesn't want to do it anymore. The Woman has become tired of playing the roles. She sees the problems it creates in her life, and she feels dead inside from constantly living in self-protection. The Woman wonders what happened to her along the way; when did she lose herself? How did she get here? She feels stuck on autopilot, going through the motions of life with little joy or happiness. She lives in a state of burnout, overwhelm, and exhaustion, doing everything for everyone except herself. She feels resentful, bitter, and angry. She looks in the mirror and doesn't recognize herself.

The Woman longs to feel free, happy, and alive, but she can't remember how. She's tired of abandoning herself over and over, putting everyone else first, feeling afraid all the time and beating herself up for every little mistake. She's tired of feeling shame and guilt. She's tired of hating her body. She feels trapped in her life but has no idea how to escape. If she gets still and quiet, she can hear a tiny distant voice that sounds vaguely familiar, like a foghorn sounding in the distance, but she can't make it out. It's too far away.

So now it's a war between the Woman and Hurt Girl. The Woman wants to be free, but Hurt Girl keeps messing things up, playing the roles, keeping the peace, not rocking the boat.

Who's going to win?

Will the Woman find a way back to First Girl, unlearn all the fear and abandonment, and remember who she really is?

Or will Hurt Girl win, and the Woman stays afraid and disconnected, putting others first and living the rest of her life in sadness, hurt, and anger?

Every Woman has a Hurt Girl inside who did what was needed to survive. We all have our own version of this story, and yet we all have the same battle going on inside. As young girls, we are vulnerable to the messages we get from our parents, teachers, friends, school, religion, and society about what it means to be female. These messages tell us who we need to be in order to be loved and accepted. We take in these messages, and then we adapt to fit in. If the message is "Get good grades," you become a great student. If it's "Good girls are seen and not heard," you become quiet. If the message is "Take care of your brothers and sisters," you become the responsible one.

If you had traumatic experiences when you were a child, then your Hurt Girl is even stronger and louder, keeping you safe in so many different ways. It might look like anger, fierce independence, disconnection from your emotions, defensiveness, combative communication, or you may be totally shut down.

It's time to go on a rescue mission to free First Girl from exile. We're going to go find her in the closet, remove the duct tape from her mouth, and bring her into the light. Then we're going to give her a seat at the table. She's going to get a voice again, and you're going to create a safe space for her to speak up. First Girl is going to remind you of your creativity and your playfulness. She'll show you how to have fun again, and how to be silly and excited about life. She is the road map home to yourself. Hurt Girl will be able to relax, put down the sword and shield, and relinquish control. Then, you, the Woman, will be in charge. You'll be able to connect to your power, stand in the awareness of your true identity, keep yourself safe, create healthy relationships, and live as the strong, independent, courageous person you were always meant to be.

Your story matters, and as you go through this book, I will help you use your story to find yourself again, uncover all the magic that got lost when Hurt Girl took over, and write a new story for yourself. Trust the journey; I've got you! Consider me your tour guide through the wilderness back to your True Self.

I'll be sharing about my relationship with Hurt Girl, and how I helped her feel safe enough to let me go back and rescue First Girl and bring her into the light. I'm going to tell you about how I stopped abandoning myself and started putting myself first and how that changed everything about my life in ways I could never have predicted.

I'm also going to share the lessons I've learned along the way and how you, too, can change your story, stop abandoning yourself, heal the scared little girl inside, and find yourself again. You'll see why being selfish is your inner GPS, your guidance system to life, and how putting yourself first will change everything and finally bring you the life you've been longing for. The life you deserve is waiting for you – a life full of happiness, peace, love, and excitement – and together we're going to make it happen.

Each chapter is divided into three sections:

- The first section is where I tell the story of my Selfish Year (you may find parts of yourself in there too).
- The second section, "Selfish Strategies," is where you'll find action steps and guidance to take into your life right now.
- In the third section, I tell the stories of some of my clients – remarkable, inspiring women who have done this work and experienced truly incredible transformations. There's so much power in knowing you're not alone, that other women have walked this road, and if they can do it, you can too. (Names and details have been changed for anonymity.)

If you feel like you're wandering alone in the desert, wondering how the hell you got here and unsure of the way out, this book is for you. If you look in the mirror and don't recognize the face looking back, you're in the right place. If you're ready to do the work to unlearn the lies that told you that you aren't enough, or you're too much, and you're ready to excavate the old shit you've been carrying around for so long and free yourself from the burden of living a life that you think you "should" be living and start designing the life you're meant to have, this book is for you.

Let's take the journey together, shall we?

Introduction

The shiny hope of a new year full of unknown potential is like a drug. It offers the opportunity to put the old year to bed, tucking in all the successes and failures, the decisions we made that worked out, and the ones that didn't. Every tick of the clock counting down to midnight moves us further away from regret and into possibility. Slate wiped clean, journal put away, photos moved to an album titled *The Past*. I love the dopamine hit of making vision boards and setting intentions, the opportunity to start fresh and hit the reset button.

It was New Year's Day 2020, and I sat in the back of a taxi on the way home, after a hasty departure the day before and a sleepless night at a hotel. If there was ever a year for a fresh start, this was it.

My husband, Leo, and I had been living in Valencia, Spain, for the past two years. We'd impulsively moved there after traveling around Spain and falling in love with the

xv

laid-back vibe, friendly people, affordable lifestyle, and stunning architecture. One hot afternoon in Seville, we'd sat in a plaza drinking cold beer in the shade of a red awning and talked it through.

"We need to shake things up," Leo said, as church bells chimed two o'clock. "If we just go back to our regular lives, we'll get complacent. Moving here will get us out of our comfort zones."

"True," I said. Our relationship was built on the mutual desire for growth, and that meant we were always looking for the next challenge, the next opportunity.

"Let's try it for a year," he said. "We have some money saved up, and we can work online." He turned to me, sweat beading on the bridge of his nose. "Look, if we don't like it, we can just move back to Canada."

Why not? I thought. *What's the worst that could happen?*

My three children had recently moved out, and I felt ready for something new. We had just gotten married the year before, and I felt a wild thrill at this new life before me. The only decision left; where? Seville was known for its summer heat, and as much as we loved it, we wanted to live near the ocean. A quick Google search brought up Valencia. Beaches – check. Affordable – check. Beautiful – it's Spain, come on. Check. It didn't take long to find an apartment, sign a one-year lease, get our visas in order, put all our stuff in storage, and begin a new adventure.

One year later, we had just moved into a new (to us) apartment in the historic center of the city, brought home a sweet boxer puppy, Lola, and finalized a two-year extension of our visas. Outwardly our lives were a storybook romance: Two sad divorcés meet and fall head over heels in love. They elope in Rome on a late October afternoon and move to Spain. Mornings are spent working, afternoons slip away at a little café by the cathedral, or while riding bikes to the beach. They make love under the Spanish moon with the windows flung wide. And they lived happily ever after.

Behind those windows, however, a very different story unfolded, one that led me to that New Year's Day of 2020, heading home after spending the night alone.

New Year's Eve at a hotel alone is pretty depressing. Add in the fact that I'd run away from my life the night before after yet another argument, and you get the idea. Me, sad and angry, nursing a glass of Rioja at the bar, surrounded by families, couples, and friends laughing, wearing sunglasses in the shape of "2020" and popping champagne. A band played in one corner, the music getting louder the closer it got to midnight. I left before the countdown started, ordered room service, and sat on the hotel balcony, eating a steak and watching the fireworks at midnight, each *boom* vibrating in my body like a wake-up call for how far my life was from what I'd imagined, and how close I was to falling apart.

I left early the next morning, checking out in the quiet lobby still decorated with balloons and streamers. I flopped into the taxi and willed the driver to slow down so I could enjoy my last moments alone before facing the reality of a life I'd fully participated in creating and now longed to escape.

Orange trees, heavy with fruit, lined the streets; men in suits weaved through traffic on motorized scooters; old women chatted on sidewalks, arms full of purchases from the market. My stomach twisted with anxiety; I wasn't sure what I'd be going back to. This wasn't the first time I'd sat in taxis, or Ubers, or on planes, running away from my life. Tension would build between us, fights would break out, and silences would drag on until I couldn't be there anymore.

I'd retreat for a few days, nursing my bruised heart, trying to make sense of how we'd gotten into this mess so quickly. Then I'd return, sheepishly hoping that the break would give us a reset, or at least that my departure would shock us both into jumpstarting our relationship so we could get back what we'd had in the beginning: love, trust, and respect.

However, I realized that although a few days away might help me think more clearly and have space away from conflict, it did nothing to resolve the deep, foundational issues in our marriage. It was a Band-Aid approach, and I knew I was just biding time, avoiding the tough conversations we needed to have that neither of us wanted.

One thing that became evident during my stay at the hotel was how isolated I had become. I had only made a few friends since moving to Spain two years earlier. Even though I'd been taking Spanish lessons, I was nowhere near fluent enough to connect with the locals, most of whom did not speak English. The people we'd met were great, but considering the tense state of our relationship, spending time with other happy couples wasn't my idea of a fun evening.

I was also in the empty nest phase of parenting, and it was rough. My youngest son had moved out at 18, far younger than I'd imagined. I felt a lot of guilt about it; at the time, I'd been caught up in my new relationship and excited to travel and elope in Italy. My son had volunteered to move in with his sister at her apartment across town, and I'd thought this was a brilliant plan for everyone, but now, looking back, I wasn't so sure. The kids supported my decisions, albeit sad that they wouldn't see me get married, and encouraged me to spread my wings.

They'd come to see us off at the airport with our huge suitcases, mine filled with the gorgeous wedding dress

I had spontaneously bought just a couple of weeks prior, and when I broke down in tears, they gathered around me and reassured me that they would be just fine.

As I walked to the security gate and looked back at the three people I'd carried in my body, birthed, raised, and given everything to, I felt a piece of my heart break. I didn't know when I would see them again. Watching them standing there, arms around each other, I hoped they would be okay.

What I didn't anticipate was that I would be the one who wasn't okay.

Walking into our apartment in the late morning sunlight on the first day of 2020 – what I hoped would be a great year (it had to be better than the dumpster fire that was 2019), I dropped my bag on the floor and kicked off my shoes. Leo and Lola were out, most likely on one of their many walks in the neighborhood, looking for the perfect place to do her business. Lola had a favorite spot that we'd dubbed Shit Alley and we spent many an early morning and late night there, willing her to relieve herself so we could go back to bed.

I sank into the sofa, relishing the stillness. It was rare to get the apartment to myself because Leo seldom went out these days and spent most of his time on his phone or staring at the walls.

We had been trying to build a life coaching business together, and most recently our focus had been on coaching couples. The irony of this was evident given the state of our marriage, and I didn't feel right helping others create a healthy relationship when ours was anything but. Neither of us was busy with clients. I didn't have the energy or focus to work on a business, and the more we tried to work together, the wider the disconnection grew between us.

I felt trapped inside our home, which made me feel guilty because I was well aware of the privilege that allowed me to have these feelings. But I couldn't shake it, and what made it worse was that he loved being together all the time and couldn't understand why I didn't.

Missing the kids became more than just a longing but a full-blown heartache. Every day, I walked around with a knot in my stomach. I'd been trying to arrange video calls once a week, but the Wi-Fi hadn't been connected since we'd moved in two months ago. We were waiting for some magical wiring to be done in the building and until then we had minimal data. I resorted to going to the lounge at the hotel across the street and using their Wi-Fi for my client calls and to talk with the kids. With the time difference, my evening was their morning, and they were usually busy.

I'd always made my primary relationship the center of my life, looking to my partner for all of my needs. Leo was my best friend, so why did I need any others? However, it became evident just how much that factored in when I didn't feel safe going to him with how I felt. I wasn't close with family, or at least close enough to open up about what was happening. So I kept living in isolation, trying to survive on my little island of one.

The problem with isolation is that you're left with your own thoughts, and they are not to be trusted. I felt so confused and overwhelmed that I didn't know which way was up. I'd normalized what was going on between us and minimized the impact. I'd gotten really good at putting on a smile and shifting the focus to everyone else.

My frantic need for time to myself prompted me to rent an office in a coworking space in the city's center. I rationalized it by seeing it as a way to focus on my own business, which I had a secret longing to grow. I fantasized about having a coaching practice of my own, where I could call the shots, make all the decisions, and unleash my creativity. I also needed the Wi-Fi for client calls because the noisy hotel was not a great option.

Every day I packed my laptop and headed to the office in the late morning. As soon as I turned the corner from our building, I would light a cigarette. I had smoked a little at the end of my first marriage as an act of rebellion, freedom, and — let's face it — stress relief. Now I found myself back in that familiar place, and the cigarettes returned. The act of lighting up, inhaling the smoke, and walking the streets felt liberating. I also felt guilty but ignored that as best I could. It was my one secret pleasure, and I enjoyed the hell out of it. Then I would sit in the tiny windowless office, do my client calls, halfheartedly work on some social media content, and then walk home, chewing gum and spraying myself with perfume in hopes that he wouldn't notice the stale scent of smoke on my clothes.

Two things happened in the next week that would shake me out of my confusion and isolation. The first was a yearly catch-up call with a small group of girlfriends. We had met and bonded when we attended a leadership retreat through the same company where I'd gotten my coaching certification. It was held at a beautiful ranch in Sonoma, and we'd all met for a week at a time, four times over a year. The act of gathering together for intense personal work and growth over that year had forged strong friendships. The five of us were scattered across the globe, but if nothing else we got on a Zoom call at the beginning of each year to check in and catch up.

One thing we always did on our call was to share our word for the year. This idea started in the backyard of the home I'd raised the kids in (the house where my first marriage had exploded – more on that later). I'd gotten the house in the divorce, and now I was getting married again. These dear friends traveled to be with me for my bachelorette party, just a few months before Leo and I were due to leave on our trip to Italy to get married.

We'd toured wineries, ate in great restaurants, and sat for hours catching up. The last morning, we gathered in my backyard, basking in the warm sun, sipping coffee, and chatting.

"Imagine where we'll all be in a year," Elizabeth said, her long brown hair shining in the sunlight. "What will we be doing?"

Each of us shared what we imagined for ourselves in the next year. We shared visions, hopes, and intentions, and one word that represented it all. My word for that year was Abundance. Other words floated in the warm summer air: Gratitude. Peace. Creativity. Reverence. I sat in my pajamas, listening to these brave, beautiful women share their hearts, and felt the warmth and safety of this small circle of people I was lucky to call friends.

We agreed to meet in a year and see if our intentions had come true. And when we gathered on a Zoom call a year later, we were surprised and delighted to discover that many, if not most, of our declarations had happened. Not in the way any of us could have imagined, and we delighted and celebrated the wonder of what we had each created in our lives. We declared ourselves the Witchy Women, and agreed to continue the ritual and meet again at the beginning of the next year and every year afterward.

That week of January 2020, we'd arranged a Zoom call to connect and share our word for the year. I'd thought about it for weeks leading up to the call. The future seemed foggy and unknown, and although I tried to muster up

Introduction   xxiii

some kind of word that felt exciting and real, it was like searching in the dark for a doorway.

What word reflected the future I saw for myself? Happy? Grateful? Free? Every word mocked me and sent me spinning into deeper despair. None of my friends knew about my situation, but they knew me well enough to know when I wasn't being authentic. I couldn't show up and fake it with them.

That morning as I waited to get on the call, one word kept resonating in my mind. I tried to avoid it, because the word didn't make sense, nor did it even seem appropriate as a word to focus on for the year. But as much as I tried to land on something that felt better, more positive, or acceptable, I couldn't shake it.

Selfish.

I kept hearing it inside my head. It began getting louder and more resonant.

I tried to talk myself out of it.

This must be wrong. Who wants to be selfish?

Even thinking it brought up guilt and shame. I'd been raised to be self*less*. The church my mother took me to every Sunday had taught me that being selfless was an honorable thing. The good girl I'd been raised to be had taken pride in her ability to put everyone else first. It was the noble pursuit, the honorable choice. *Selfish* was a dirty word, something that we called people who were vain, narcissistic, arrogant, and only interested in themselves. Why would I ever aspire to that?

Selfish was reserved for women who discarded others, only spoke about themselves, and didn't care who they hurt in their pursuit of attention. Hurt Girl knew, to the core of her being, that you never acted like that. She knew that in order to survive, you made damn sure everyone else was happy, and that the very idea of putting herself first was a great way to be rejected, ridiculed, and abandoned.

And yet I couldn't let it go. Something inside me kept repeating it, like a heartbeat.

Selfish. Selfish. Selfish.

I began to get curious. *What if this is my word for the year? What if everything I did, every choice I made, I did because it felt right for me, and for no other reason? What if I put myself first, listened to my intuition, trusted it, and acted on it, for an entire year?*

Something inside of me stirred. I felt a deep resonating thrum and a shiver of excitement radiated through my body. I didn't know what it meant, but I felt like I needed to trust it. It scared the shit out of me, which told me there was probably something here, and I felt more connected to myself in that moment than I had in a very long time.

Dialing into the Zoom call, I felt my heart pounding in my chest. *Was I really going to declare this? What would my friends think? Shouldn't I pick a better-sounding word? A more spiritual one?*

With shaking hands and shallow breath, I looked my friends in their faces on the screen of my laptop, and said the words.

"My word for 2020 is Selfish. For one whole year, I will only make choices that are right for me, that feel good for me, that my intuition guides me to. I don't know what that will look like, or how I will do it, but that's my word." I paused, feeling like an idiot for saying it out loud, wishing I could take it all back.

"I love it," Elizabeth said.

"Me too," Zee chimed in. "Can't wait to watch what happens!"

"Sounds pretty powerful," Tyi said. "Keep us posted!"

Introduction xxv

I looked at their faces on the screen, each one smiling back at me, and I felt the collective energy filling me up. Their support, their unconditional love, radiated into my heart, giving me a tiny bit of courage and hope that I might be onto something. I hung up the call feeling like something had changed. I didn't know what, but I felt a shift inside, like I'd moved some things around and made a bit of room for something different, like those puzzles where you have to slide pieces around to make room for the right piece to fit in the right spot. It felt like I'd moved something aside, and something had opened up.

Little did I know, this one word would change everything.

The second thing that happened that week was a conversation with my best friend, Samantha. I'd been holding back from sharing with her about what had been going on because I didn't want to burden her with my problems, and did my best to keep things light and happy on our calls. This had created distance between us because the effort it took to pretend everything was okay was enormous, and I wasn't being fully myself with her. Our relationship was more surface than I wanted it to be.

I called her that week and opened up. I told her what I'd been going through, and let my emotions surface. As uncomfortable as it felt to let her see my pain, I briefly caught her up to my situation. I could see her face change as I got honest with her. As much as I didn't want to "complain," I had nobody else to talk to.

"Val, I'm worried about you," Sam said, her forehead crinkled as she peered into her phone. Even from all the way back in Canada, I could tell she was taking this seriously. "I think you should get out of there for a bit. Why don't you come back to Canada for a while? Hang out with your kids? Some space might do you good."

"I don't know, Sam. We just got Lola, and she's a lot of work, and I haven't even unpacked from moving into the apartment.. . . I don't know if now is a good time." I could hear myself making excuses.

Hadn't I just declared this my Selfish Year?

Sam frowned. "Please just think about it, okay?"

I promised I would. Sitting in my office after the call, I checked in with the place inside me where the word *Selfish* had come from. If I really meant what I'd said to my friends, and I was going to make every decision for the entire year based on what felt right for me, it had to start now.

I peeked deep inside and asked, *Do I stay, or do I go?*

The answer came immediately.

Go.

Chapter 1

The Sofa of Truth

Chapter 1.

The Sola of Truth

The Spanish sun lit up the bedroom like a jewel as I lay in bed with my first coffee of the day. It had been three weeks since I'd returned from the hotel on New Year's Day, and one week since I'd made the "Selfish" declaration to my friends. Since then, I'd spent my time hiding in the bedroom, going for long walks through the city, and trying to erase the whole thing from my mind. I felt stupid and ashamed that I had even thought about being selfish. *What right do I have to complain? To be sad?*

The doors to our small balcony were open, and I could hear the soft staccato of mothers chatting with their children as they walked them to school. A dog barked in the distance and the bells of the church down the street told me it was nine o'clock. I lay back on the pillows and wondered, like I had every morning for the past few months, how I'd gotten myself into this mess.

I slid out of bed and passed the master bath with the gleaming copper tub we'd had shipped from England. Our 10-week-old boxer puppy, Lola, gave a woof from her crate in the corner, eager to be let out.

My bare feet felt warm against the herringbone hardwood as I passed through the living room into the kitchen. The main living area was one large room divided by a massive brick pillar, flanked on the street side by two French doors with their original wood shutters, and on the other side a large window looking into the courtyard of the building.

Leo sipped an espresso on the huge leather sofa we'd bought in Madrid. He didn't look up as I walked past; the silence in the apartment sat in stark contrast to the street noises outside.

"Morning," I said as I rinsed out my cup.

"Morning," he replied.

4 THE SELFISH YEAR

My stomach tensed, but I tried to ignore it and focused on wiping the counters. In the hallway outside our front door, I could hear workers setting up for the day. They'd been restoring the original tiles on the stairs, and every day as I walked down the three flights to the main floor, it looked more and more like I imagined it would have in the early 1900s, when the building had housed just one wealthy family.

The day loomed ahead of me, and I wondered what to fill it with. I had a few client calls and then a big empty void on the calendar. Normally that would excite me – a day with nothing to do – but these days it filled me with dread.

A familiar tightness gripped my chest and I leaned against the counter, studying the back of my husband's head, wondering for the millionth time how we'd gotten here. Not just in Valencia, as two Canadians who'd put everything in storage and moved, sight unseen, to a rental apartment in a city we'd never visited. Not just in this beautiful apartment that we'd bought on a whim and spent the last six months renovating. I wondered how we'd arrived at this place in our relationship. How did we stray so far from that heady day two years ago when we got married in Rome, feeling the October sun on our heads as we promised to love each other for the rest of our lives?

We'd bought the apartment in the spring of 2019 after a whirlwind romance, an Italian elopement, five months of travel, and countless impulsive decisions. The building had once been a grand manor and, like everything else in Valencia, what you saw on the surface hid centuries of history underneath. First, the Moors built their city, baths, and temples. Then the Romans came and built on top of that, and their first road lay under our bedroom. Across the street, the Roman Circus once hosted the elite of the city, who

The Sofa of Truth 5

came to watch races and shows. Afterward, the Christians showed up and built on top of the Roman city, creating the cobblestone streets, grand cathedrals, and churches that stood outside our windows.

The manor had been divided into apartments, and ours was on the third floor, looking onto the street in the front. It had been stripped down to the original brick, concrete floors, and traditional curved ceilings so common in Spain. Over the course of six months, we'd brought the place back to life, restoring the original brick walls wherever we could, placing new glass in the French doors of the three balconies, and bringing our mutual passion for design into every detail. It should have been a dream come true and yet, as we worked together choosing tile samples, lighting fixtures, and furniture, I felt numb and disconnected. I couldn't get excited about the process. Leo questioned me about it.

"You don't seem into this," he'd said one evening as we looked at furniture online.

"I am," I said. *Lies.*

"You're not excited about the process. In fact, you seem annoyed most of the time."

I fell silent. He was right, and I had no good answer. Here we were, planning a trip to Madrid to pick out a sofa, and I could barely muster up a smile. The only thing I thought I felt was exhaustion – another lie. The truth was that I really felt an ocean of emotions; I just wasn't prepared to acknowledge them.

I couldn't see a way out of the life I'd created, and this made me feel trapped, scared, and ashamed that I even felt that way. As a life coach of seven years, and after over a decade of working on myself, I knew logically that I wasn't stuck. I could reason with myself and think through my options, but every time I tried to do this, my fear shut it down hard. I ended up in confusing loops in my mind that paralyzed me and convinced me that I had no choice but to stay in the mess I'd created.

I had a lot of reasons to stay right where I was. We had only been married for two years; we'd had a dream wedding, just the two of us, in Rome and the photographs were like something out of a magazine. We'd rented a classic car and had a driver take us through the ancient city, the golden sun warming our heads as locals shouted "*Auguri!*" ("congratulations" in Italian) as we drove past. Cruising past the Colosseum in the gorgeous dress I'd brought over from Canada, next to my best friend, on our way to get married in the original *Campidoglio* (city hall) felt surreal.

We'd met when I was newly single after divorcing my first husband and father of my three children. I'd met husband number one when I was 18; he'd proposed after three months of dating, and we were married one year later, two weeks before I turned 20. Naive, confused, and swept off my feet by his grand gestures and dynamic personality, I fell into marriage like a skydiver falling out of an airplane: loving the free fall, praying the parachute would open. I saw marriage as an easy escape route from living with my parents. He had ambition and drive; I had a desire to be rescued. He wanted to be an entrepreneur and real estate investor; I wanted to go along for the ride. He was outgoing, fun, the life of the party; I was shy, introverted, and insecure. This guy was everything I wasn't; maybe he could fill the missing pieces inside of me. I went full-on Jerry Maguire. You. Complete. Me.

As a young and naive girl, I quickly figured out the formula to make our marriage work. People-pleasing saved me, just like it always had. Hurt Girl knew what to do.

The Sofa of Truth

Stuff my feelings, repress my anger, and be selfless. Sacrifice my career for his. Give up my financial power to him. Lose myself in parenting and running the household. Be a good wife and make everyone happy. Keep the peace. Be the buffer. Shape-shift to accommodate.

What I didn't know back then could fill an entire book. I didn't know that he had bipolar disorder, and a growing alcohol addiction. I didn't know why our life descended into chaos over and over. I didn't know that my Hurt Girl, and his Hurt Boy, were running our lives. And I didn't know that we were on a slow train to disaster.

Twenty-four years later, our marriage screeched to a dramatic ending (more on that later), and I realized that not only was I not complete, I'd become a shell of my former self.

A mere three months after the end of my marriage, I downloaded a dating app and threw together a profile. Hurt Girl would not allow me to sit in misery. The pain I felt from witnessing my marriage end felt insurmountable. Add to that the pain of my three kids as they processed their parent's divorce, and I was sinking fast into darkness. Instead of taking time to heal, Hurt Girl came up with a brilliant plan: distract, avoid, deny. I told myself that I would just "see what's out there" and have some fun; *didn't I deserve that, after everything I'd been through?* I further justified it by reminding myself that husband number one and I had been separated three times, seen four different therapists, and had been trying an in-house separation over the past year. I'd felt alone inside the marriage for a very long time. So I bought into Hurt Girl's logic.

Leo was the first guy I matched with on the app. He was handsome, with kind eyes. Good banter. He asked me out and I said yes, in spite of that little voice inside whispering, "Are you out of your mind?!"

Our first date was a walk with my dog. I felt nervous, worried that someone would see me, and doubting my decision with every step we took on the path along the river. Hurt Girl was calling the shots, but my denial wasn't so deep that I couldn't see that this was probably a very dumb idea. I'd even asked my therapist what he thought about it, and to my surprise, he'd given me the green light, with a disclaimer.

"You've done a lot of work on yourself already, Val," he'd said when I asked if he thought I was ready to date. "I think you're ready. However," he paused and leaned in. *What, however? I met a great guy and he makes me laugh and my insides are nothing but dark tar after the hellish year I'd had. I don't want a "however."*

"Don't ever lose yourself in a relationship again."

I leaned back and smiled. *Easy.* After all the trauma of my first marriage, there was no way in hell I would ever abandon myself again.

I dated Leo in secret for a few months; the kids were still reeling from their dad moving out, and I didn't want to introduce someone else into their lives yet. I liked the secrecy; he'd leave flowers on my lawn with love letters and my favorite chocolate. He'd put cards and notes inside my mailbox. I'd tell the kids I was going for a walk and run down the street to meet him in his truck and we'd drive and talk. I felt like a teenager, addicted to the thrill. He left flowers on the windshield of my car when I was at work, and we'd meet on the beach to watch the stars. After decades of neglect and loneliness in my first marriage, it felt like water in the desert — an oasis of love, care, and attention. He worked night shifts as a nurse; I'd drop the kids off at school, go to his basement apartment, and crawl into the warm bed, where we'd make love all morning. I fell hard and fast.

One evening, we lay on the couch together at his place watching my favorite movie, *Eat Pray Love*. He was the big spoon. I loved the feeling of being engulfed in his arms.

"I think God brought me into your life to heal you of all the men who've hurt you."

It sounded so lovely, the way he said it. At the same time, something twinged in my gut. *Did I really need a man to heal me?* I pushed the thought aside and nestled deeper into his arms as Julia Roberts slurped spaghetti in Italy.

Lesson: Your intuition always knows the truth, and yet so many of us have been taught to ignore it, especially if it goes against what others want. Perhaps you've gotten used to ignoring your own discomfort, in order to make others comfortable. As you learn how to tune into your intuition, you'll start to trust yourself to know what's right for you.

Now, our Spanish dream had become my nightmare, and I reeled at how two good people with good intentions could hurt each other to such a degree that we were left confused, devastated, and wary, circling each other like the gladiators had in the ancient Roman Circus across the street. We'd gone from best friends to shells of our former selves, choosing silence as the better option so as not to ignite another daily battle.

I couldn't imagine leaving but couldn't bear to stay.

One of the most frustrating things about this was that I thought I'd dealt with all of this already. Ten years of coaching clients, working on myself in therapy, and having a coach myself, not to mention being married to a coach, had made me a bit of a self-growth snob. I pranced arrogantly into my second marriage and the expat life, believing that I had it covered and that I knew how to navigate whatever might come my way.

While that's partly true, it's also partially not true. I got caught up in my ego, which told me I could handle this massive life change with expertise and that it would only bring me more joy and love than I ever imagined because I'd already done "the work."

What I didn't see – my most significant blind spot – was that the partner I'd chosen was the perfect person to trigger all of my hidden issues that required deeper levels of healing. I was asleep to my deeper layers of trauma, and while I sauntered into Spain with all the confidence of a bullfighter, I was about to be dealt a fatal blow, one that would gut me to a level I'd never before experienced. And the bull I fought was myself: my pain, trauma, subconscious beliefs, and Hurt Girl were about to rear their heads.

I was asleep to all of this like a first-class passenger on the *Titanic*; blissfully unaware that a cold, dark death was imminent and unavoidable, sleeping under cozy blankets of denial, and failing to see the reality of my situation.

The iceberg that woke me up wasn't awareness. It wasn't reading a book that revealed my deep level of self-abandonment. It wasn't the constant fighting, or silent treatment, or endless conversations about what was happening and why. It wasn't listening to a podcast or talking to a friend or going on a retreat. I did all of those things, and none of them were the iceberg that crashed the deep levels of denial about what was really going on.

The iceberg – the big, hulking, destructive, shattering, immovable force that shook me awake – was pain.

The pain of staying in a relationship that felt like an open wound of loneliness and abandonment. The pain of waking up every morning and feeling the self-hatred of failing at being a good partner. The pain of isolation from my children, family, and friends. The pain of walking through a city where I didn't speak the language – in spite of hiring a private tutor – and couldn't connect to people in any real way. The pain of drinking bottles of wine every evening, alone in my room, trying to soothe the void inside. The pain of pretending to my clients that everything was fine, trying to build a business where I was meant to be an inspiration, and feeling like a fraud.

The pain was the iceberg under the surface of the water, dark and looming, coming closer and closer to shattering my life that was loosely held together with coping mechanisms, denial, fake smiles, and alcohol.

I remember the day the iceberg of pain shattered my illusions and fantasies, and I fully woke to the truth: that I had, once again, abandoned myself to keep the peace, not rock the boat, and not have to face Hurt Girl.

It was in the middle of the night on my sofa in Spain.

We'd had another fight, where we'd both said things we didn't mean and let them hang in the air, un-take-back-able. Lola whimpered in her crate, and I whimpered in the bed. Finally, I couldn't breathe in the hurt-filled air anymore, so I grabbed my pillow and a blanket and went to the sofa.

It wasn't the first time I'd done this, and it hurt just as much as all the other times. I lay in the dark, stared at the ceiling, and wondered where it all went so wrong.

This time I didn't just go back to sleep and wish it all better the next day as usual. This time, I experienced something that I can only call a phenomenon. After enduring the same thing over and over, after hours, days, weeks, months, and years of having the same conversations, nothing changed. And after continuous attempts to fashion myself into the version that would fix what was broken, it happened. Like a clock ticking over to a new hour, I felt something shift inside.

The level of pain scared me, and I felt like if things kept going as they were, I might not make it out alive. I could feel old dark thoughts circling the edges of my mind, thoughts about what it would be like to just stop existing. I knew I would never act on it and never had before, but the awareness that these thoughts were creeping back and lurking in the shadows terrified me. I had let myself get to a dark place, and this time something told me that it had to be the last time.

I laid on the sofa until dawn, going over and over in my mind what to do, how to fix this mess I'd created, how to change it. I wanted to feel happy again. I wanted to feel alive again, and I didn't know how to get it back. I was so far down the rabbit hole, I couldn't see daylight anymore.

That's the tricky thing about rabbit holes. We burrow so deep into the darkness, it feels like we've been swallowed alive. Consumed with worry, fear, and confusion, we can't see any way out. And yet, there always is. The light is still there, the sun still rises every morning. Our job is to look up, find the tiniest glimmer of light, and follow it.

Selfish Strategies

Have you had a sofa moment? Have you had that dark night lying awake, with only the sound of your beating heart and your terrified mind? Have you felt the pain of staying stuck, and have you reached a point where the pain of staying where you are is bigger than the fear of change?

It took me 49 years to get there. Some people never get there. I'm guessing if you're reading this, you're close, or you're already there. You're opening to the idea that there's more possible for you, and you're wondering if you could have what you've always wanted. Maybe it's freedom from fear or self-loathing. Maybe it's a healthy relationship with someone else, or a healthy relationship with yourself. Maybe it's a successful business, or the ability to travel whenever you want. Maybe all you want is some goddamn peace and quiet and room to think. Or you may not know what you want yet, but you sure as hell know what you *don't* want.

What's your sofa moment? What do you lay awake at night thinking about?

It's time to get real with yourself about what you're no longer willing to tolerate and why. It might be just one area of your life that needs to change; it could be every area. Maybe it's your health; you're sick and tired of feeling sick and tired. You long to spring out of bed with energy and excitement for the day ahead. It might be your finances. You want to create financial freedom so you can travel when and where you want, or buy that house you've been dreaming about, or send your kids to college. Maybe you've given financial responsibility to your partner, and you're ready to take it back. You want to experience the pride and satisfaction of earning your own money. Or maybe you've lost yourself along the journey of life. You put the kids, partner, family, job, duties, and responsibilities before yourself, and now, decades later, you look in the mirror and don't recognize the person looking back at you. You've lost your mojo.

I posted a video on TikTok and talked about the "sofa moment" that so many women experience. I asked my community to share their sofa moments, and the comments were astounding. Thousands of women shared their own version of the sofa moment and how long it took them to get there. They talked about their experiences fighting for the change they needed for years, sometimes decades. They shared stories of emotional abuse in their relationship, toxic family members, persistent health issues, and debilitating financial stress. And they talked about their sofa moment; that time and place when the switch flips, and they're done. Some could vividly remember the exact time and place when they felt it.

Listen to these women's voices and see if you can find yourself in their stories.

> "I was on the edge of that moment for at least a year, and then a consequential conversation pushed me closer. One morning, I woke up with a visceral knowing that this ends today. It's as memorable as our wedding day."
>
> "Once I explained the definition of abuse and asked him to stop hurting me on purpose, I was done the very next time he hurt me. I no longer have tolerance for anyone hurting me anymore."
>
> "I'm done with my mother. Done being treated like crap and people saying 'but she's old, she's your mom' – but she doesn't respect who I am."

Women are resilient. We don't give up easily, and we fight for what we need and know is right. It's pretty incredible, isn't it? We can endure suffering, pain, heartache, and stress and still keep going.

It's also our Achilles' heel. We stay too long, bend too far, give too much. We care for everyone else until we're a dried-up husk of our former selves.

Kenny Rogers said it best: "You gotta know when to hold 'em, know when to fold 'em."

Your sofa moment is not a defeat. You're not giving up, and it's not a failure. It's sacred.

The Sofa of Truth

It's that moment in time when your soul speaks to you in such a way that you can no longer ignore, deny, distract, and avoid what She's saying.

Your soul slaps you awake.

Here's what your soul might be saying:

"Bitch, no more! You've been trying to change this for so long and nothing's happening. You've been putting up with this situation, trying to make it work, doing everything you can think of. You've been sitting on the fence, hoping that things will magically change. You're avoiding facing the truth, avoiding facing yourself. You know what needs to change. You know what's wrong here. You know that you've been letting fear run the show. You know. Not choosing is choosing. It's time to pick yourself up off this goddamn sofa, stand tall, and choose yourself."

Wherever you're at, waking up is the first step.

We fall asleep to ourselves in lots of ways. Denial, coping mechanisms, numbing, stuffing. Addiction, distractions through kids, partners, friends, shopping, media. Routines, patterns, and work. Even fun things like travel, parties, socializing, and decorating our houses can become convenient ways for us to stay asleep.

I used to be addicted to shopping. For a couple of years, I bought something every day. I bought stuff I didn't need, didn't want, never wore, and certainly couldn't afford. But it gave me a rush of excitement and anticipation that filled a void inside. It scratched an itch I wasn't even aware I had. It gave me something external to focus on, so I didn't have to look at myself.

Waking up to yourself requires that you start by asking yourself some tricky questions. This is where you're going to practice giving yourself lots of compassion and

16   THE SELFISH YEAR

grace. As you wake up to all the ways you've put yourself last and abandoned yourself, it doesn't do any good to beat yourself up about it. So kick your inner asshole outside for this next part.

Grab your journal. Don't have one? You've got your first homework assignment!

Buy yourself a journal just for this work. Find one that speaks to you, looks pretty, or feels special. Your journal will be your new best friend, your confidante, the place where you will find yourself again.

Many of my clients feel nervous about journaling because they're afraid someone will find it and read it. If that's you, I encourage you to do what you need to do to feel safe. It's important that you can write, uncensored, unedited, raw, and real. The act of putting pen to paper is ideal; there's something powerful that happens when you experience this visceral act. However, if you know that you won't feel comfortable enough to let loose on the page, try an online journal such as www.penzu.com. It's free and password protected.

If you've never journaled before, or the last time you did was your "dear diary" teenage ramblings, keep an open mind and try going through my journal prompts. These prompts are designed to connect you to yourself in new and deeper ways. If it feels uncomfortable or challenging, remind yourself that growth happens outside of your comfort zone, lean in, and keep going. I promise it will be worth it.

1. Find a picture of your First Girl, who you were before you were told you weren't okay. If you can't find a picture or don't have one, write out a description of what you imagine she was like. What is she wearing? What does she love to do? See if you can connect to her.

The Sofa of Truth   17

What does she feel? What's she like? Is she quiet, or boisterous? Thoughtful, or spontaneous? Funny? Curious? Write out as much as you can.

2. Now find a picture of your Hurt Girl. Who you became after you were told you weren't okay. Again, if you can't find a picture, imagine what she's like. Now ask yourself the same questions. Whatever her age, connect to her and listen.

3. Consider all the ways you're asleep to yourself. Remember, this isn't your fault! It's a normal coping mechanism when you've learned that who you are isn't okay. But now it's time to take a look at the patterns and behaviors that are keeping you numb and distracted from what's really going on. Make a list of everything you notice about how you keep yourself from the truth. Here's a list of some common ones to get you started:

> Shopping
> Food
> Alcohol
> Drugs
> Social media
> Watching news
> Reading
> Crafts
> Socializing
> Work
> Travel
> Moving
> Exercising
> Diets
> Spirituality
> Religion
> TV

Isolation
Medication
Self-help books
Podcasts

None of these are wrong or bad and lots of these are great. These behaviors only become a problem when you use them as ways to avoid looking within at the truth of how you really feel, avoiding your pain, and keeping yourself from acknowledging the hurt inside that you don't want to look at. So again, bring that compassionate self to this exercise, and know that we all have a list.

If you're feeling heavy, or you're noticing that this is bringing up some stuff that is painful, remind yourself that this is normal. It's always darkest before the dawn, and I promise you, if you stay with me on this journey, you'll be so glad you did. You've got this!

Also, here's a little tip: If at any time you feel like the work is getting too heavy or too much, take a break and shake it off. You're bringing old energy to the surface that's been buried for a very long time, and as it surfaces, it's important that you let it move through you.

Play a song that you love, one that makes you want to move. Get up and dance! Move to the music, groove to that song, and let your body show you what it wants to do. Maybe your body wants to shake, stomp, or sway. Really get into it and feel your body releasing this energy. When the song is done, take a moment to be still, close your eyes, and notice how you feel. Does your body feel tingly, or maybe lighter? What do you notice?

Now thank yourself for showing up, and go do something nice for yourself! Have a bath, make some tea, go for a walk – whatever makes you happy.

Client Story

Sarah came to me for coaching because she was curious about the process and wanted to see if there was something in it for her. She didn't feel like she needed help or that she had anything to work on. She felt pretty satisfied with her life, and happy overall. She asked for one session just to try it out because she was in a place of exploring and trying new things.

In that first session, I took her through an exercise that had her examine different areas of her life, and rate them 1–10 based on her current level of satisfaction. We spent some time talking about her health, spirituality, where she lived, her relationship with her husband and her family and friends, her finances, career, and personal growth. Sarah's numbers were pretty high to start with, eights and nines. As we continued to talk and explore, and I began to ask deeper and more probing questions, her numbers began to drop. She started to look deeper into herself than she ever had before, and to wake up to how she really felt. She had been living in denial. She'd been people-pleasing her entire life and her childhood had been extremely chaotic and unsafe. She had excellent coping mechanisms in place that had kept her safe as a child, and now they were keeping her from her truth. She'd locked her heart away and had been living from her head. Her almost complete abandonment of herself had kept her in almost total denial of how she really felt, and the reality of some of her situations. Her Hurt Girl was running the show, and it looked like chaos, depression, anxiety, conflict, and drama. First Girl was nowhere to be found. She'd been locked away decades ago because it had never been safe for her. She went into hiding and Sarah had no idea where to find her.

(continued)

(continued)

As Sarah continued to look deeper at her life, and deeper within, she began to wake up to the truth – that she was miserable. Her marriage was a constant cycle of conflict, and she didn't feel seen or heard. She hadn't had sex in years and felt alone and abandoned. Her relationship with family was full of drama and chaos. Her children were in various stages of dysfunction and she was constantly rescuing them from their problems. She'd lost her business and finances were a disaster. She was depressed and could barely function each day, let alone take care of things like paying taxes and cleaning the house. Her health was suffering; she had no energy to exercise or eat well. Her thoughts were torturing her with self-loathing, hopelessness, despair, and constant criticism of everything she did.

By the end of our session, her numbers had dropped to the bottom: one to three in every category.

Sarah was shocked. She'd just woken up in a dramatic fashion. It was like in The Wizard of Oz, *when Dorothy arrives to see the wizard, and she's watching with awe and wonder. Then Toto pulls the curtain and she sees the little man, pulling levers and pressing buttons. The illusion is shattered and she sees that it's all just pretend.*

Sarah saw for the first time that she'd been in such deep denial that she'd believed the illusion that Hurt Girl had created. I explained that this was created so that she could survive. It was exactly what she needed at the time, in order to cope. Only now, it wasn't serving her, it was killing her. And it was time to pull the curtain back, expose the facade, and get real.

Sarah and I worked together for three years. I showed her how to connect to First Girl and create a safe space for her to have a voice again. We went deep into the beliefs and patterns that Hurt Girl had established and began to dismantle them. Sarah built her courage over those three years, and step by step, began to cultivate new beliefs that aligned with the truth: that she is brave, powerful, and loving. She learned how to set healthy boundaries with her family. She practiced asking for what she needs with her husband. And as she applied the Selfish Strategies, she started falling in love with herself more and more.

In that time, I witnessed her transform into a woman who is a total badass. She has faced herself and the truth. She worked tirelessly to rescue First Girl, bring her back, and help her to feel safe. She learned how to love herself and make choices that work for her and to recover from people-pleasing. She became a better wife and mother and now enjoys a loving relationship with her husband and children. She has set solid boundaries with her family. She found a job she loves and is working toward starting her own business.

Sarah began putting herself first and finally getting real with herself and doing the work to heal, and it gave her everything she didn't even know she wanted and needed.

Chapter 2

Rock Bottom

Chapter 2

Rock Bottom

Remember I said that a new year is like a drug for me? The potential, the unknown, and the promise of a fresh start light me up like the fireworks at midnight. Unfortunately, that drug has a kicker; the excitement of new beginnings comes with a deep need for constant change and restlessness that kept me in cycles of drama. And, like most drugs, the high was worth the low, until it wasn't. This year, the lows were becoming lower than I'd ever hit before, and the highs were starting to feel less and less exciting. I didn't know it at the time, but I'd become addicted to drama, turmoil, and chaos. It felt like shit, but I needed it to feel alive, and the pattern wasn't new.

Two years earlier, I'd found myself in the same pattern, but in a different country. This time it was Mexico, at the end of 2018, and the addiction to chaos reared its head like clockwork.

I'd walked along a beach in Playa del Carmen, barefoot, sandals in one hand, bag slung over a shoulder. The sand felt like powdered sugar. To my right, the turquoise waters of the Caribbean glistened in the afternoon sun, the surf pounding a steady rhythm that soothed my nerves.

Inside my bag, I had my phone, journal, and a pen. I was searching for the perfect spot to meditate, get quiet, and clear the thoughts out of my scrambled brain.

Leo and I had been traveling since September. We'd lived in Florence for a month and Rome for a month, got married in Rome, then visited Greece, Marrakesh, and Spain. Seville captured both our hearts, and we wandered the small streets, marveling at the orange trees heavy with fruit. We sat in the sun and drank in the energy of the people. Everyone seemed so relaxed and happy compared to Canada, and we spent hours sitting in plazas watching families, seniors, and young people hanging out, chatting, and laughing. We then moved on to Barcelona, where we roamed the Gothic quarter and sat in cathedrals in silence, watched flamenco dancers in dark, crowded rooms, and fell deeper in love with the country.

Afterward, we planned to spend the winter in Mexico. We'd booked a small suite at a hotel near the main street in Playa del Carmen, a block from the beaches and all the action of the tourist center.

It sounded like a great plan: take a break from celebrating Christmas and spend it on the beach instead. After years of creating the magic of Christmas for the kids, I felt exhausted just thinking about buying presents and decorating a house. I loved it when the kids were little; seeing their eyes light up at the tree and experiencing the wonder and excitement through them was worth all the work. Now that all three kids were living on their own, I found myself longing to skip the entire holiday and all the pressure and demands it brought. I felt disillusioned by the whole thing, and "skipping Christmas" was just what I needed.

It seemed like as soon as our feet hit the sandy beaches, our relationship hit the rocks. We fought over everything and couldn't seem to find any solid ground or sense of safety, and the dramatic increase in conflict bewildered us both. Every day we attempted to start fresh, and every day would end in a fight. Leo began sitting out by the pool in a deck chair for hours, listening to audiobooks and staring into space. *To escape me*, I imagined. I watched him from inside our tiny suite and felt so confused. The man I loved seemed to have no idea how to connect with me, nor I with him. I felt hurt, angry, and confused.

New Year's Eve was a turning point. We'd had another stupid fight, and I stormed off, wandering the streets full of partying tourists, feeling like an island of misery in a sea of celebration. I wished for the thousandth time that I was anywhere but there. The happy glow on everyone's faces made it even worse, and the contrast felt depressing. As I passed families laughing, couples toasting with champagne, and friends spilling out of bars and restaurants, I sunk further into myself.

I'd finally run out of energy to be in the streets and returned to our suite. It was empty, so I sat in the dark, listening to the fireworks as midnight arrived and 2018 began — a new year and yet I felt more desperate and scared than ever. Leo came back shortly afterward, and we went to bed in silence. There was nothing to say.

One week later, there I was, looking around for a quiet spot on the beach to journal and meditate. I navigated to a quiet area with shade from nearby palm trees, sat on my towel, and opened my journal. Looking out at the ocean, my thoughts wandered, inevitably landing on my new marriage that was drowning fast.

I couldn't help but think that this was all his fault. He wasn't communicating; his silence was more painful to me than shouting, and he'd started getting more and more frustrated with me. I tried to appease him, to connect with him, to say and do all the right things, only to end up right back where I started.

As much as I knew that it took two people to create a problem in a relationship, my thoughts kept going to blame. I couldn't get past his actions and behaviors to see my own, and I felt confident that if only he changed, everything would be fine.

It didn't matter that I'd been a coach for 5 years, or that I'd worked on my healing and growth for 10 years, or that I'd read dozens of books on relationships. It didn't matter that this was my second marriage, that my first had exploded, and I'd gone deep into therapy. It didn't matter that I knew blame never worked and focusing on his actions would be futile. It didn't matter that I'd spent the four years we'd been together working on taking ownership of my issues and how I contributed to the problems.

Our conflict triggered trauma from my childhood that I thought I'd healed. I was in almost constant fight-or-flight mode, and the only thing I could see was that I didn't want to be there. I looked around me at the pristine beach, turquoise waters, and gulls swooping on the breeze.

I'm the luckiest girl in the world.

Get me the fuck out of here.

However, instead of picking my self-pitying ass off the hot sand and booking the first flight home, I sank into one of my oldest and most familiar comfort zones.

People-pleasing.

Looking back, I can see this as yet another abandonment of myself and what I knew in my gut to be true. But it's hard to see ourselves in those times when we shift into old patterns of coping. At the time, it feels right, because it's giving us some sort of relief from the pain of the situation. In the moment, I believed that if I shape-shifted into what I thought Leo wanted or needed, I could make the pain stop. I knew how to disappear, shut down my intuition, and say or do whatever was necessary to make him happy. I'd been doing it most of my life. Hurt Girl was an expert at it, and if there were a degree out there for people-pleasing, I would have a PhD.

I grabbed my bag, stuffed my journal and phone inside, and walked back to the hotel.

I didn't notice that the tide had risen since I'd been sitting there. Three feet of water blocked the route I had taken

Rock Bottom 29

to get to this spot. The water surged around a large boulder I had skirted to get to the beach. Eyeing the waves crashing against the boulder, I considered whether I could navigate through them to the other side, where the beach widened.

A man stood behind the boulder and motioned me to walk toward him and through a private resort to avoid the swirling water.

I shook my head at him and plowed through the surf. Something in me needed to prove to him, and myself, that I could do it.

Almost immediately, the powerful surf knocked me off my feet. I landed on my ass, submerged up to my neck, my bag soaked.

I crawled the rest of the way as the guy laughed at me, shaking his head at my stupidity. I made it around the other side of the boulder and emerged, dripping wet and humiliated. Pulling my phone out of my bag, I tried to dry it off with my wet T-shirt.

> Lesson: Women are so resilient, aren't we? We're masters at putting our heads down and doing what needs to be done. And yet this often leads us to making things harder than they need to be. Sometimes life offers us an easier path – one that would require us to lay down our resilience and receive support – and instead we say, "No thank you, I'll take the hard way." Watch for the helpers along your path, and see it as an opportunity to practice receiving.

Walking back to the hotel, I was quite a sight, in my wet clothes, hair dripping, and feet squishing in my flip-flops. I didn't care. I was furious with myself for making such a stupid decision that ruined my phone, which I had only bought recently. I got back to our room, threw everything on the couch, peeled my wet clothes off, and got in the shower.

As the hot water washed away the humiliation and frustration of what was supposed to be a peaceful morning, I couldn't help but notice the irony of my situation. If I'd listened to that guy showing me the safer route, I would have saved myself the embarrassment and saved my phone as well. Instead, I went barreling ahead into the choppy waters, needing to prove myself, in some way, that I knew best or that I didn't need anyone to help me or tell me what to do.

And look how that turned out! More evidence that I couldn't trust myself, that I didn't know what I was doing, and that I didn't have the answers. I saw it as a sign that my decisions were shit, and confirmation that I should follow Leo's lead, let him make the decisions, and trust his judgment over my own.

Sitting by the pool that night, still smarting from my beach failure, the subject of moving to Spain came up again. We'd been going back and forth on it for weeks. He wanted to do it, but I wasn't so sure. The more I stalled, the higher the tension got, and I'd been feeling the pressure to make a decision. We went over the pros and cons again, and he reiterated what he'd been saying all along: It would be a great adventure, get us out of our comfort zone, we would grow a ton, and it would shake up our small and predictable lives we'd both been living.

I felt a bone-deep, full-body exhaustion that took away any desire to try and figure out what I wanted anymore, so I said what I knew he wanted to hear.

"Let's do it. Let's move to Spain."

His eyes lit up. "Really? Are you sure?"

I swallowed the truth, which was that I wasn't sure at all. I didn't want to leave my kids, I felt scared and overwhelmed by the idea, and the amount of work it would require to get visas and figure out the logistics exhausted me just thinking about it.

"I'm sure," I said, thinking of the guy at the boulder, shaking his head at me. *What did I know anyway?*

This moment started me on a whole new level of self-abandonment and kicked me back into old patterns of putting others' perceived wants and needs before my own to keep the peace. I saw it coming like the surge of surf around the rock, and yet, just like when I plunged into the waves and got knocked on my ass, I saw the danger and waded right in.

For the next two years, I sunk deep into people-pleasing, abandoning myself, appeasing, jumping through hoops, being nice, and being whoever I needed to be to avoid conflict and avoid disappointing Leo. I stayed in those choppy waters of self-doubt, tossed around and feeling like I was drowning, doing my best to get through it but sinking further beneath the surface all the time.

I made decision after decision that I knew deep down weren't right for me. Big decisions, like moving to Valencia, starting a business together, buying our apartment, and getting a puppy, seemed obvious. But the small ones were almost the worst. Those were the thousand daily deaths that beat me down and kept me depressed, isolated, and numbing out. I swallowed my opinion, had sex when I didn't want to, told him what I thought he wanted to hear, pretended I was okay with him walking out or being silent, believed him when he said I was the problem, and acted happy when I was miserable. Those were the small deaths that led to the big ones. Every day, I abandoned myself in some small way, and two years later I had diminished myself to a kernel of truth surrounded by a field of lies. I couldn't find myself anymore. I'd been buried beneath the ground, cold and dark and alone, and no amount of digging could unearth me.

I knew I had a choice. Three choices, actually. One: stay down. Give up, lay down, and accept that this was my life. Let Hurt Girl win, and succumb to the daily deaths. Two: Sink deeper. Fully give up and give in to the darkness and let it win. Three: Rise up. Find a shovel and start digging my way out. No shovel? Use a teaspoon and excavate myself from the rubble, one spoonful at a time.

Selfish Strategies

Seeing fault in everyone else is a lazy way to live. It lets us off the hook for our reality and places the blame on others because it's easier than looking inward and asking ourselves some tough questions. It's easier than facing some painful truths about ourselves.

It's also been programmed into our subconscious that when things go sideways, look for the culprit. The man/boss/friend/parent/money/society is to blame, not us. We get to stay in victim mode, feel sorry for ourselves, and expect something outside of ourselves to change. Then we can have/be/do what we want.

People-pleasing is a slippery slope. Get out of one victim role, and we think we're free for good. Then before we know it, another relationship or situation comes into our life with just the right recipe of codependent fuckery, and we slip on the victim suit again like a cozy sweater that feels so comforting and familiar. It's like the arcade game Whack-A-Mole. Just when you think you've smashed the victim part of you, it pops up somewhere else, and it can take a while to recognize that you've put the suit on again.

So, how do we get out of the victim trap? How do we extricate ourselves when it's so familiar to blame others? What do we do when we find ourselves, yet again, looking at everyone else, expecting, waiting, hoping, and praying for them to change, so we can finally be happy and free and have the life we want?

I like to call it *radical responsibility*. It's the perspective that we are responsible for ourselves, our choices, and our reality, and that is all we are responsible for. We aren't responsible for anyone else, their choices, attitudes, or emotions.

It's the way out of the endless loop of victim/blame/shame/guilt that we build for ourselves.

Radical responsibility means acknowledging that your job is not to caretake others' emotions. Your job is not to change someone else so they fit neatly into your plans. Your job is not to wait for someone else to come and save you.

There is no one coming to save you; you must save yourself.

Radical responsibility is the way you become your own hero.

It means that you look inward and acknowledge that you've been operating out of a place of pain, trauma, and fear, and that you will do the work to heal. It means that you trust that you have all the answers inside of yourself, even if you can't see it yet. It means that you will take ownership of the life you've created, the relationships you've chosen, the experiences you're having, and the choices you've made. It means that you will no longer abandon yourself for anyone else, that you will learn how to connect with your true self, that you will do the work to love yourself again, and build the courage to make choices that come from your inner being.

Radical responsibility puts your inner being in the driver's seat, and we lovingly move Hurt Girl into the backseat. She doesn't get to drive or navigate anymore. It means that you commit to going on a journey of self-discovery so that you can take back your power.

Radical responsibility doesn't let others off the hook. It means that you set rock-solid boundaries with love, respect, and grace and that you teach others how to treat you in the way you deserve. It means you make tough decisions about who stays in your inner circle and who goes. It means you have uncomfortable conversations when needed, design new alliances with those closest to you, create emotional safety for yourself and others, and be willing to walk away when something or someone is no longer the right choice.

If you're in a tough spot right now, if you're looking around at some of your situations and relationships, and you're seeing that you've made some choices that didn't reflect your highest good, remind yourself right now that it's okay. You're not alone in it. It's okay not to be okay, and it's time to stop the blame game and begin to take ownership of your life. You're ready, and it's time. The only thing standing between where you are now and where you want to be is radical responsibility. It's the key to unlocking everything you want.

The first step is acknowledging that you've been playing the blame game. You see that you've abandoned yourself in some way, that you've believed that it's because of someone or something outside of yourself and that you've felt powerless to change. This can be the hardest step, because victim mode is so subconscious. It's not like we wake up every day and tell ourselves, "Today, I'm going to be a victim, give my power away, and stay stuck in this shitty situation."

Most likely, we wake up and say, "Today, I'm going to do my best with what I've got, power through, keep my head down, and survive."

So it takes a lot of intention, grace, and compassion with yourself to look at your situation or look at the areas of life you aren't happy about and see how you are the master of your reality. It takes a lot of courage to be willing to acknowledge that victim mode has been a way to abandon yourself and deny the truth of what lies deep in your heart.

Here are some questions to help you lovingly look inward:

What areas of my life am I dissatisfied with and do I desire to change?

Rate each area on a scale of 1–10, with one being very dissatisfied and 10 being very satisfied.

____ Emotions
____ Thoughts
____ Relationships
____ Finances
____ Career
____ Parenting
____ Family/friends
____ Spirituality
____ Physical environment (where you live, your city, your home)

Of the areas where you want to improve your satisfaction level, write out what would make this area feel like a 10 for you. Get specific. How would you feel? What would it look like? Where are you? What are you doing? Who are you surrounded by?

In each area, remove the external factor. If it's a relationship, remove all focus on needing your partner to change. If it's your career, remove the need for your boss, coworkers, or situation to change. If it's family, imagine that family member never changes.

Then, ask yourself these questions:

How are you contributing to the situation?
How are you showing up that's not working for you?
If you solely focused on yourself and changing how you show up, what would that look like?
If nothing outside of you changed, what would you do differently?

One thing that helped me when I was doing this inquiry was to remind myself that regardless of the situation, I always had a choice. Being in victim mode convinces us that we are powerless, we don't have a choice, and we are stuck. This is never true. Stuck is a perspective.

Shortly after leaving my first marriage of 24 years, I went with my daughter to a tattoo parlor and had the word "choice" tattooed on my left wrist.

This word holds so much meaning to me because it was the realization that I always had a choice that gave me the courage to leave a marriage that was toxic and abusive.

Even if I couldn't take action at the moment, I could choose a different perspective.

Here are some suggestions of where you can choose radical responsibility:

Choose to think different thoughts, which generate other emotions.
Choose to reach out and ask for help.

Rock Bottom

Choose to remove yourself from a situation.

Choose your words and actions.

Choose the meaning you placed on whatever was happening.

Choose to believe the best in yourself and others.

Choose to set a boundary and enforce it.

Choose to take care of your emotional, physical, mental, and spiritual needs.

Choose to detach and disengage.

Remind yourself that no matter what's going on, you have choices. Write a list of choices you have in your current situation. This doesn't mean you have to act on any of them. All you're doing is exploring what you could choose if you wanted to. There's power in naming it.

What can you choose?

_____

_____

_____

_____

Once you see that you are showing up as the victim in some way, and you can acknowledge that while it's worked for you in the past – hell, it helped you survive – it's no longer serving you, it's not working, and you're ready to let go of that familiar role, you are ready to take radical responsibility.

I'm going to give you what I like to call the *Radical Responsibility Recipe*. When you put them all together, the ingredients help you to take back your power, put you back in the driver's seat of your life, and get you moving in the direction you want to go.

Radical Responsibility Recipe

1. What *don't* you want? There are things you may no longer be willing to tolerate in your life. Maybe it's a relationship or some habits that aren't serving you. Dynamics with family members or friends. Drama and chaos. Emotions, like sadness or anger. Your financial situation or your current job. Maybe you just don't want to cook dinner every night. Make a list and let loose. Get in touch with everything you no longer want. This isn't about complaining or being ungrateful. It's about getting clear with what you've allowed into your life that you're ready to release or change. (Don't worry; we'll get to what you *do* want a bit later. It's a lot easier to figure out what you want when you get clear on what you don't want!)

2. Beside each item, write out how you've been contributing to it. Where have you been lacking boundaries, allowing mistreatment, or not speaking your truth? Have you been in avoidance, denial, or stuffing? Angrily confronting? Blame? This is the time to bring your gentle observer and get into it. Yes, it's uncomfortable ... but the only way is through it and you can do it!

3. Beside each of those, write out what you could do differently. How could you show up in a way that honors your true self? What is one thing you could change about the way you're engaging in this situation that would feel more true for you? Maybe it's having an uncomfortable conversation, or writing an email. Maybe it's making a micro change in a habit, like going for a 10-minute daily walk or starting a journaling practice. This is where you show up bigger for yourself, even by 1%, so that you can start to see how powerful you truly are to change any

circumstance. Maybe you want to research going back to school, or starting a business.

4. Now make a commitment to yourself to take action on some of these steps. You get to decide what you're ready for, but I challenge you to commit to taking action on *one* step for each item. I promise you this will make a huge difference. These small steps will build the foundation for bigger changes and as you go through this book, this will build momentum.

Please take a moment and fill this out. It's such a powerful step that tells your subconscious that you mean business. You are showing up for yourself, and while it may seem silly or inconsequential, I promise you it's not. You're taking your power back, in a very real way, and it's one of the big steps to freedom and the life you are meant to have!

Commitment:

I,_____, commit to taking these action steps.

_____

_____

_____

_____

I commit to taking Radical Responsibility for myself, and to always look for where I have choice. I trust that as I take these steps, I am walking myself into the future that I truly want and deserve.

_____

Signature

_____

Date

Client Story

Julia came to me on the heels of a major financial loss, the breakdown of her marriage, toxic relationships with her family, and months of depression. She spent the first few sessions talking about it all, as if no one had ever listened to her before.

As her story unfolded, it became clear that Julia was deep in victim mode. And while it was true that the people in her life had been treating her horribly, it was also true that she was allowing it. She'd been taught from an early age that her opinion didn't matter, her voice didn't matter, she didn't matter. She'd been treated as an afterthought, as someone whose sole purpose was to take care of others. No one had ever modeled what it looked like to have emotions and process them in a healthy way, or what a good relationship looked like, or even how to have an opinion and stand up for herself.

When we see someone acting in ways that continue to sabotage their happiness, their relationships, finances, health, and value, it's easy to ask, "What's wrong with her?"

But the better question is "What happened to her?"

What happened to Julia is that her First Girl was annihilated by judgment, criticism, hatred, attack, abuse, shame, guilt, and neglect. First Girl went deep into hiding because it wasn't safe to be her. Hurt Girl surfaced, the one that knew what was needed to survive, and she did a great job.

Hurt Girl is the one who adapts. She knows that in order to survive and stay safe, she must comply. She must stay silent, keep her head down, make sure others are happy, and do what she's told.

It's what got Julia through her early years.

Now, as a 43-year-old woman with a husband and two teenagers, Hurt Girl was creating havoc.

As we worked together, Julia began to see how this had played out in her life. She started to wake up to the idea that while what happened to her was terrible and she didn't deserve any of it, she was now an adult and it was time to take responsibility to heal and step into the power of her true self.

This takes time. It takes time to unravel the past, to see that what happened to her wasn't her fault, even though she's paying the price for it every day. It takes time to stop feeling like that Hurt Girl, hiding in the corner, powerless over what's happening. It takes time to see how victim mode is not serving her. It took time for Julia to be willing to stop blaming everyone else, and open to looking within at how she was stuck in victim mode.

It took Julia a full year to get to the place where she was ready to acknowledge that she was in victim mode. It took time for her to see that she had choices and could make change, that she wasn't powerless over how others were treating her anymore. That she was no longer that little girl who couldn't say no. That she was now a grown-up and her radical responsibility was to heal Hurt Girl, to go back and give her what she never got, and to help her to feel safe so that she didn't keep creating chaos.

Julia worked with me for three years, and I watched her transform from angry, bitter, resentful, scared, hurt, and powerless into happy, free, open, loving, and connected. I watched her face her past, heal, and forgive, and then turn to her present with clarity, take responsibility for her situations, and begin to change them. She worked on becoming a better communicator with her husband. They started couples therapy,

(continued)

(continued)

and he began working on his issues as well. They now have a loving and healthy relationship. She learned how to set boundaries and began teaching her family how to treat her. She had to end relationships with some of them. She stopped enabling her children, stopped rescuing and fixing, and instead began teaching them how to be independent adults. The more she stepped into her own power and responsibility, the more her children did the same. She got a new job doing what she loves and is working toward starting a business.

When I asked Julia what her biggest lesson has been over the last three years, this is what she said:

"I've learned that nobody is coming to save me. I had to do it myself. And when I finally stopped looking outside myself for the answers, or to be rescued, when I stopped needing everyone else to change, and started working on changing myself, I realized that I'm powerful. That I can change my life by changing me. And that changed everything."

Chapter 3

Running Back to Myself

Chapter 3

Running Back to Myself

It was a few weeks into my Selfish Year, and I still hadn't made a decision about what to do next. *Do I stay, or do I go?* Being selfish was still a new concept, and while it felt true in my gut, my mind held on to people-pleasing like a steel trap. I couldn't think my way into feeling good about leaving my marriage, my home, and the country. It didn't matter how I tried to justify it; I always ended up back in guilt and shame, like a traffic circle I kept driving around and around and never taking an exit. Guilt was my familiar place, my comfort zone. And yet deep down, I knew I was simply killing time. Every evening I would open up Expedia and look at flights to Vancouver, imagining myself getting on a plane and going back to the West Coast. I could smell the salty ocean air and the mossy trees, where I'd spent almost every summer growing up. Our family vacations were road trips south from our small town in northern British Columbia, to the coastal city of Vancouver, then on the ferry over to Vancouver Island. The ocean, the mountains, and the old-growth rainforest were my happy place, and now it was my obsession. I dreamed about sitting on rugged beaches and walking the woods, ferns brushing my ankles as I passed by. It became a yearning, a pull that grew harder and harder to resist, despite the guilt that kept me tethered right where I was.

Something had to give.

I'd had so many breaking points over the two years we'd lived in Spain. And yet, because I considered myself "strong" and "resilient" (my name, Valerie, literally means "strong"), I didn't completely break; it just created fissures that I tried patching over and ignoring.

One of those fissures happened shortly before we'd moved into our new apartment. We were still in the rental, on the outskirts of Valencia, and the stress of taking on a mortgage in a foreign country to purchase the new place was affecting me more than I cared to admit. I tried to discuss it with Leo in hopes of getting some reassurance, but our conversations would end in constant fighting, name-calling, and silent treatment (on both sides). I couldn't think straight. Just when I felt clear in my mind, we'd sit down and talk, and hours later we'd still be talking, and I'd feel confused again. More and more, we'd spend an entire day talking, taking bathroom and food breaks, until the day was over and we were right back where we started, only exhausted shells of ourselves, staring at each other with haunted eyes.

I couldn't be in that space for one more day, so I booked an Airbnb for a week. I'd found a little apartment in Rusafa, a trendy neighborhood a short walk from our apartment, that looked like a good place to land.

I told him my plan with a shaking voice.

"I just need some space and time to think." I couldn't look him in the eye. I felt like such a failure.

He said he understood and watched as I climbed into a taxi with my duffel bag.

Sitting in that little apartment on the second floor of a quaint building overlooking a vibrant street corner, I felt numb. I could hear tourists at the Mexican restaurant across the street, children playing, and dogs barking. The lilt of Spanish floated into the window. I watched the sun move in shadows across the wood floor until it got dark and evening came.

I peeled myself off the tiny couch, moved to the bed, and slept.

The next day, I ventured out and bought a few groceries, then came back and sat on the couch again.

What am I doing? I felt stupid and ashamed, worried about Leo and how he was doing, and a little shocked at what I'd done. Watching the sun move across the floor again, I noticed a ringing in my ears and wondered how long it had been since I'd sat in a quiet room alone.

The French philosopher Blaise Pascal famously said, "All of humanity's problems stem from man's inability to sit quietly in a room alone."

I'd been running from that quiet room my whole life. I ran from my parent's rooms by getting married at 19 and lived in rooms of chaos and turmoil. I distracted myself in the busy and joyful room of parenting three kids. I followed my first husband from room to room, moving more than 20 times, making money just to lose it again, and spending decades in a distracted jumble of confusion. I jumped right from the rooms of a divorced single mom starting a career, to the rooms of a second marriage. All the rooms of my life had been full of convenient distractions from myself.

This time, for the first time in my life, I sat quietly in a room alone and didn't run away. This time, I didn't distract myself with food, alcohol, men, or moving. I just sat there and felt the discomfort of facing myself.

Lesson: Spending time alone, with no distractions, can feel uncomfortable (even scary) if you've never done it. This is when all those thoughts and feelings you've been avoiding rush to the surface. And yet it's the only way to truly get to know yourself. Your answers lie within; when you commit to solitude, even just ten minutes a day, you'll be amazed at what you discover.

48 THE SELFISH YEAR

As I let my thoughts float around without trying to make sense of anything, I slowly noticed space opening up inside my mind.

I fed myself. I slept.

The next day I opened my journal and started writing.

Monday

I'm sitting here by myself not to escape, but because I feel a deep need and longing to come back to myself. I don't feel strong enough to do this when I'm with him. I'm too wrapped up in the relationship to know my truth.

This was so fucking hard, leaving for an entire week. But I can't do it anymore.

The last month has been horrible. I feel so lost. I have zero motivation. No energy. Depressed. Anxious. Adrift. Fighting all the time.

I see myself being reactive, angry, blaming.

I don't know who I am. I'm floundering, failing, and feeling desperate.

Tuesday

I want connection but am also afraid of it. When things are really good, it feels amazing — but it never lasts. Something will happen that makes me feel unsafe and then I retreat, push away, isolate and attack.

I love being in a relationship but also fear it. I fear losing my identity because I never really had it to begin with. How can I maintain something I never found?

And so I blame the relationship.

I blame him.

I feel trapped and smothered, and at the same time desperately want love and acceptance.

I want to forge my identity, but I don't know how.

I make choices and then regret them. I'm always looking for something else.

I spend my days distracting, numbing, and avoiding.
I'm terrified to make changes that I know will help me.
So where do I go from here?
I love him. I want to make this relationship work.
I just don't know how to be me inside of it.

Wednesday
I'm at a crossroads. I have everything, so why am I so discontented? I've forgotten the fundamentals of happiness. It's like the Universe is trying to teach me the same lesson over and over and I keep failing the test. But what even IS the fucking test? To learn how to create happiness within myself? It seems like this should be easy . . . but every time I fail, the consequences get bigger.
Staying in this life feels unbearable, but leaving is unimaginable.

Thursday
The only distance between us is a few miles, and yet it feels like oceans. Can I find my identity and keep my grasp on it, while I'm inside this relationship? I want to. And yet this space serves me. I feel an opening. A crack in the armor. I was created as a spiritual being. My Sacred Self is within me and always has been. She is the best part of me. She knows the way and knows the truth. Every time I lose sight of her, I give my power away. I must connect with Her until SHE becomes ME. That's where my power lies, where all my dreams are waiting to become real.

The longer I sat in the silence, the more I saw how I'd been sabotaging myself. I realized that blaming the relationship, or blaming Leo, had become a convenient excuse for abandoning myself. The fog started to lift and I could see myself as separate from him, and I began noticing how much power I'd given away.

He didn't take my power. He never wanted it. I freely and willingly gave it away by disconnecting from myself and attaching to him and trying to get my needs met from the relationship. I felt so angry with myself. Here I was again, after all those years of working on my growth and healing from the codependent mess from my first marriage. I thought I'd overcome this pattern. And yet sitting there in a rented apartment, a few minutes' walk from the life I'd chosen and worked so hard to build, I was not only right back there, but deeper than ever before.

One week later, I took the short cab ride back home and walked through the doors once again. I felt hopeful that my time away was enough to change me, to remind me of my power and strength. I prayed that I could make things better, that from now on things would be different. I found him in the kitchen, making dinner: pasta with a rich bolognese sauce, fresh bread from the corner bakery, and a leafy green salad. A bottle of red wine gleamed in the decanter, and blues music filled the air. I dropped my bag in the entry, walked into the kitchen, and threw my arms around him, breathing in his earthy, familiar scent. He wrapped his arms around my waist and kissed my neck.

I sent a prayer into the warm Spanish evening, asking for the one thing I'd been searching for my whole life and had yet to find – myself.

Selfish Strategies

Giving away your power is an insidious process. It's not like you woke up one day and told yourself:

> "Today, I'm going to give up my autonomy, abdicate my personal authority, and give someone else the power to determine how I think, feel, and act."

It goes more like this:

"I love this person; I want them to be happy, and I don't want conflict or for them to feel uncomfortable or disappointed in me."

Or, even more likely, we have zero awareness that we're doing it. It's completely subconscious and, therefore, far more dangerous.

Giving away my power felt like pulling on an old sweater: familiar, comforting, and safe. In reality, it's none of those things. The very opposite, really. It's the most unsafe thing we could ever do. Giving away our power puts us in dangerous territory. We become vulnerable to others' intentions, motives, desires, and decisions. We're swept away into someone else's story, playing a supporting character, standing in the shadows so the other can shine. And we do it willingly, albeit unconsciously. We become the masters of our own demise.

Why do we do this to ourselves? When did we learn to give away our power?

Women are told from an early age that who we are isn't enough, and that we need to be someone else in order to receive approval and love.

We're told:

> Be the good girl. Be nice. Smile. Look pretty. Don't get dirty. Get good grades. Don't offend anyone. Don't have emotions. Don't have opinions. Be modest. Be polite. Don't talk about money or sex or politics. Be sweet. Hug your creepy uncle. Stay home while your brother gets to do whatever he wants.

We watch:

> Pretty girls get praised. Smart girls get praised. Athletic girls get praised. Skinny girls get praised.

We are told we are too:

FatThinPrettySexyPlainLoudCrazyEmotion-
alQuietSillyOpinionatedBoyishGirlyAngrySad-
HappyRomantic

We are:

AbusedNeglectedBeatenAbandonedDeniedUnseen
UnheardCastAsideIgnoredBeratedLaughedAtBullied
JudgedRejectedComparedToLeftBehindDimin-
ishedMinimizedMadeWrongShamedGuilted-
CheatedOnManipulatedLiedToUsedCriticized

We are told we are not:

Sexy enough. Smart enough. Modest enough. Nice enough. Outgoing enough

We are taught that our purpose is for others' pleasure and comfort.

Every experience you've had that's taught you that who you were created to be is wrong has become embedded in your subconscious as a belief.

That belief, distilled down to one sentence?

Not enough.

It becomes a part of your identity, even if consciously you deny it. It's living in your mind, hidden in plain sight. A shadow waiting quietly, always ready to pull you back the moment you try to rise.

If you believe you are not enough, you will act like you are not enough.

One great way to act like you are not enough is to give your power away to others. It's the ultimate act of not-enoughness. The Hurt Girl says,

> "Fine, I believe it; I'm not enough. So here. Take my enough-ness. Take my power to choose for myself. Choose for me."

You may be giving your power away to your partner, or someone you're dating, or to your kids, friends, family members, coworkers, or your boss. You might be giving your power away to circumstances, addictions, distractions, and habits. There are many ways that you give your power away without even realizing it.

And moment by moment, year by year, decade by decade, those tiny abdications of power turn into a big problem. It turns into:

An unlived life. Depression. Anxiety. Health issues. Body hatred. Sadness. Anger. Rage. Bitterness. Resentment. Numbness. Overthinking. Control. Perfectionism. Procrastination. Workaholism. Avoidance. Stuffing. Distracting. Addiction. Despair. Rebellion. Fear. Helicopter parenting. Avoidant parenting. Jealousy. Comparison. Violence. Apathy. Shame. Guilt. Blame.

Until one day, a turning point arrives. In each woman's life, there comes a time when the Universe presents us with a point of no return. A time where you're at the end of yourself and desperate for change. This will look different for everyone and will arrive unexpectedly, gradually sneaking up on you until one day it's there, staring back at you in the mirror.

It might be a health scare or a relationship crisis. Maybe it's a career change or a big move. It could be the loss of someone you love or a betrayal. It could be as small as a chance encounter that wakes you up or as big as a near-death experience. Whatever it is, you'll know when it happens. It could come gradually, like a slow burn, or quickly, like a flash fire.

The key is to recognize it when it arrives, to see the tipping point for what it is, and not dismiss it like so many other times. The key is to turn toward it instead of pushing it away like you have for so long.

You may have had many of these moments, and yet, time after time, you've pulled on that old sweater of denial, wrapped it around you, and sunk into the cozy place of abandonment because that's what you were taught to do.

But one day, you won't. One day, you'll pull that sweater out and see it for what it is — an old, ugly, misshapen identity that others stitched together and told you to wear — and you'll say:

"No more. I won't wear it anymore. It doesn't fit, it's not me, and as tempting as it is to keep putting it on, I won't do it."

That's the day you start taking your power back. That's the day you realize you don't need that old identity. You, naked and raw, are enough, without all the labels, opinions, judgments, and shame. Your power lies within, and it's yours to take back or give away. Giving it away hasn't worked all that well, so you're ready to try something different.

That *something different* is holding your power inside yourself and staying with the discomfort until it feels natural and normal.

So how do you begin? If you see that you've been in "not-enoughness" and that you've been giving your power away, how do you start getting it back?

First, it's time to "sit quietly in a room alone." It's hard to see clearly when you're surrounded by the people or situations you've been giving your power to. Giving yourself time and space is essential.

Does the idea of taking time alone feel uncomfortable? *Good.* Don't run away from it. You may feel tempted to slam this book shut and throw it in a drawer. Notice the urge and get curious about it. What is it about being alone with yourself, with no distractions, that feels scary or unsettling?

Running Back to Myself

I know so many women who've never gone on a trip by themselves. They can't even imagine it. Why? Because it's uncomfortable to be alone when you've spent your whole life abandoning yourself. It's scary to think about relying on yourself for everything when you've relied on others for so long. Being alone means being with your thoughts and feelings, and if you've been avoiding, distracting, and numbing for a long time, this will feel highly uncomfortable.

You've probably heard the saying "Growth happens outside of your comfort zone." It's true. Unless you're willing to get uncomfortable, this book will get tossed aside, and you'll go back to the status quo.

It's time to get uncomfortable, remove the distractions, stop running from yourself, and get still.

I'm going to ask you to do something brave. I want you to book some time just for you. You'll know what's right. It will feel exciting, scary, and a little bit selfish (or a lot selfish). When you imagine taking this time, you'll hear all sorts of protests and excuses in your mind as to why you can't or shouldn't do this. You'll probably feel guilt and maybe some shame thrown in for good measure. That's okay! It's just your brain freaking out because putting yourself first doesn't feel safe. I assure you, this is the safest thing you may ever do. Observe your mind doing its thing, and take action anyway.

Book yourself into a hotel or a cabin for a couple of days, or even better, for a week. Take yourself to Mexico. Hawaii. Go big.

If that makes you break out into hives, take a weekend away. Book into a local hotel that has a spa. Grab a tent and go camping. Get in your car and take a road trip, stopping at a motel on the way. Get creative!

THE SELFISH YEAR

Can't do a weekend? Book a day off. Tell your husband he's taking the kids for a day and go to a park with your journal. Hire a sitter or drop the kids off with friends.

Can't book a day off? Do a half day. Stay home, lock the doors, and turn off your phone.

I'm not letting you get off the hook! This is important, and it's possible. Find a way. You must begin taking time to be alone with yourself. It's easy to make excuses to put yourself last, but that's what got you into this in the first place. In order to create something new, you will need to take new actions. The first step in taking your power back is to make time in your life to be with yourself. You can't change what you can't see, and this is about seeing and understanding.

Before we move on, I want you to commit to spending time with yourself. See it as the first step to taking back your power.

I,_____, commit to spending time alone on _____(date) for_____ (length of time).

Congratulations! You're showing up for yourself, and it will make a huge difference!

Carving out time to be alone is the first, critical step to getting your power back. Also, this is not a "one-and-done" situation. Consider taking time alone regularly. You could even choose a time each week to work through the exercises in each chapter. But for now, let's plan how to make the most of this time.

1. **Set the Scene.** Bring intention to this time, whether it's an hour, a day, or a week. Ensure you're somewhere you feel safe, where you won't be interrupted or distracted. Bring elements into your space that stimulate

Running Back to Myself 57

your senses and feel indulgent. If you're used to putting yourself last or making other people or things a priority over yourself, this may feel like a challenge. Lean into it. Go for it! Take this part seriously, and don't overlook it.

You could:

- Buy fresh flowers and set them out in a beautiful vase.
- Light candles.
- Play some beautiful music.
- Buy your favorite foods and set them out as if you had a special guest coming over.
- If you don't have a journal yet, this would be a great time to buy one that speaks to you. Purchase a lovely pen that feels good in your hand.
- Have your favorite beverage in a beautiful glass or mug.
- Wear comfortable clothes that feel good against your skin and make you feel beautiful/sensual/sexy.

2. **Reflect.** Take time to think about all the messages you've received as a young girl and growing up. This isn't about judging your parents; they most likely did the best they could with what they knew at the time. This is about your First Girl. What was she told, either directly or indirectly, about who she needed to be? Go back to the list above for help. Make your own list. Let it rip! Now is not the time to protect others, minimize, or avoid. Get it all out on the page. You can burn it after if you want, but it's important to write everything you can remember that made you believe that you aren't enough just as you are, that you needed to be someone else to be accepted or loved, that you didn't matter, or that your purpose was to make other people comfortable or happy. Write about anything that happened to you that damaged your

identity, your soul, your body, your mind. Be brave. You've got this! If anything comes up that you're not ready to acknowledge or write about, that's okay. Just leave it for now. This exercise isn't about reliving trauma; it's about reflection and introspection. So if something feels too big, scary, or painful, set it aside. Your intuition knows when it feels safe to explore and look at something, and if the emotions are too overwhelming, now is not the time. Trust that you will know when it feels safe to go there.

3. **Illuminate.** Look back over what you just wrote and think about how each of these affected your First Girl. What did she come to believe about herself because of all of this? Who did she become in order to survive? The people-pleaser, the good girl, the good student, the quiet one, the loud one, the invisible one?

How is Hurt Girl showing up, trying to protect herself? How do you see that you still live out this false identity? Remember to hold great compassion with yourself as you gently observe. Do not go into judgment. Your Hurt Girl did what she needed to do to survive. Now it's time to bring your adult self to this exercise and get curious. If you struggle to hold compassion through this exercise, simply move on to the next. Don't go down the rabbit hole of self-judgment.

4. **Recognize.** Now is the time to practice that radical responsibility from Chapter 2. Read back what you've written so far, and see if you can recognize how you are giving your power away because of what's happened to you. You are the adult now, and regardless of what's happened in the past, it's your job to heal yourself, set yourself free, and rescue First Girl.

Write out everything that you notice. Where are you staying silent so as not to rock the boat? Where are you projecting or blaming others? How do you show up when you're triggered – reactive or responsive? Do you feel like you're in victim mode? Do you feel powerless? Are you people-pleasing, being a martyr, letting others make decisions for you that go against your intuition, or going with the flow when it's not what you really want? Where do you lack boundaries, feel taken advantage of, used, or unappreciated? What are you denying yourself because you don't think you deserve it or that others won't approve? Are you keeping yourself small to gain approval from others?

Take your time. It doesn't have to happen all at once. This is your journey, and you call the shots. Just keep going, keep asking yourself the hard questions, and keep being real with yourself.

If you find it challenging to connect and find answers, that's okay, too. If you've been disconnected from yourself for a while, this is normal. Just know that even your willingness to ask yourself these questions and to sit with yourself is a huge step and one to be celebrated. Trust the process, trust yourself. Your answers will come.

5. **Commit.** By now, you can probably see why you gave your power away, and you recognize how you've been acting it out in your life.

Awareness is the first step. You can't change what you can't see, and hopefully, you are seeing how you, through no fault of your own, have abandoned yourself in many ways.

This isn't a quick fix. It's not like you can flip a switch and become empowered. It's a process, it takes time, and it will look different for everyone. You may need to find support through a coach or therapist. You might need to enlist the help of a trusted friend.

As you work through the rest of this book, you will get more tools, support, and insight on your journey to becoming the empowered, powerful, and badass woman you are meant to be. So don't worry too much about the "how" of getting your power back. This chapter is all about the "why" of it.

That being said, if you're chomping at the bit to create some change right fucking now, then go for it! Here's some ideas for you:

- Decide on one boundary you'd like to implement. It could be anything from taking regular time alone to asking the kids to help out more around the house, or saying no to the church committee who always asks you to volunteer every Sunday. If you feel ready, go for it. We will get into how to set boundaries later on in the book if you need more help and guidance.
- Decide you won't stay quiet about one thing you have been holding back on. Maybe it's talking to your mother about holiday plans, or your partner about cleaning the garage. Pick a time to have that conversation, come prepared with the points you want to make, and jump in.
- Pick one thing you've been wanting to do that is just for you that you've been putting on the back burner. Join a gym, or hire a sitter one afternoon a week so you can do whatever you want. Go out with friends regularly, or book a vacation on your own. Pick it, book it, do it.

Client Story

Marie was a mom of four young kids and had been married for 20 years to her husband, Karl. They had settled into a familiar place of raising kids, building businesses, and being involved in their community. Marie, a stay-at-home mom, devoted her days to taking care of the kids, cooking meals, and cleaning the house. In her spare time she helped Karl in his business and volunteered at their church. She felt frustrated at the lack of connection in their marriage. The kids and business were an easy distraction from the obvious fact that neither of them were happy in the relationship. Sex had become an infrequent and lackluster event, communication consisted of bickering and criticism, and time alone was nonexistent.

Marie felt exhausted and burned out. She'd forgotten what it was like to have a life of her own that didn't revolve around being a mom and wife. She felt resentful of the kids, of Karl, and of her choices. She tried to be grateful for the life she had, but couldn't get out of the depression and sadness of the awareness that she wasn't living her own life. Her life revolved around everyone else's lives. She had no time to exercise, socialize with friends, or even get regular haircuts. Her days consisted of dragging from one chore to another, driving kids around, and being everything to everyone.

Marie had given her power away at every turn. When she came to me, she was firmly entrenched in victim mode. It was Karl's fault that they never had sex and fought all the time. He was so distracted by his business. It was the kids' fault that she had no time to herself. They had so many needs and she was the only one to meet them. She couldn't see a way out, and had no hope of anything changing anytime soon.

(continued)

(continued)

And yet she came to me because in her desperation, she couldn't let go of a little glimmer of hope that there might be a solution.

As we worked together, Marie began to tell me about her childhood. She'd been raised to be a good Christian girl, to dress modestly, be quiet, not get angry, and to be modest and pure. She'd been shamed for any behavior that was outside of the rules and guilted into submission. Her First Girl had been wild and free; Hurt Girl became sullen and quiet.

Marie began to see how she'd been conditioned to put herself last in every area, and that it was the coping mechanism for strict repression and oppression.

Eventually, she realized that putting herself last was the choice she kept making, subconsciously, from the Hurt Girl place, because it felt safe. As long as she didn't make waves, have any needs or demands, as long as she kept the peace and put everyone else first, she'd get the love and approval that she longed for.

Marie started noticing how she'd been choosing to put up with the lackluster marriage. She saw how she did everything for the kids instead of requiring them to help out and take on more chores. She noticed herself saying yes to every volunteer request without even considering whether or not she wanted to.

As her awareness of how she was showing up grew, she started to see different choices that felt better.

She learned how to set and communicate healthy boundaries and began communicating them to her family. It ruffled some feathers at first, but soon everyone got on board and adjusted.

She practiced saying "no" without explaining or justifying, and felt euphoric afterward when she experienced the feeling of empowerment that came with it.

She sat Karl down and told him how she felt and that she wanted them to go to counseling. He agreed and they are working on their communication and connection.

Marie still struggles with the old conditioning and programming that tell her to put herself last and to give away her power. But every day she grows in strength and courage. Every step moves her toward herself and the life she wants to be living.

She also decided to go back to school, and her family stepped up to support her and take on more responsibilities. She feels alive again, excited about life and her future, and aware that she has the power to make choices that are best for her, and in doing so, her family is much happier and more content as they see her fulfilled, engaged, and happy. The time with her kids is better because she's fully present when she's with them. They are learning how to be more independent and responsible. Karl loves seeing his wife going for her dreams and growing in her confidence.

Marie is one badass woman and is creating an amazing life.

Chapter 4

Doorways

Chapter 4

Doorways

The first month of my Selfish Year marched to a close, and while I hadn't found the courage to get on a plane, I had taken some baby steps. I started focusing less on Leo and more on me, determined to figure out why I was so unhappy, what I needed, and how to give it to myself. Despite my fantasies of fleeing the country like a fugitive, I kept going through the motions of life each day, doing my best to be agreeable, to avoid conflict, and to put on a smile.

Pretending only takes you so far.

I slept on the couch more frequently. Feeling lonely inside of a relationship is agonizing, and I preferred to feel lonely on the couch rather than lonely in our bed. I lay awake at night, watching the moonlight stretch over the ceiling, trying to figure out how to fix this mess, how to fix me.

One day toward the end of January, I left the apartment to go for a walk. It was late afternoon – golden hour. The air felt like warm honey on my face. I turned a corner and entered Plaza de la Virgen, the beautiful square marked on one side with the Turia Fountain and at the other, the cathedral. The water in the fountain tumbled over the large statue of Neptune, and I sat on the edge, letting the cool spray land on my back. I closed my eyes, and the sound of rushing water transported me back to the Pacific Ocean and all those years I'd spent on logs, watching the waves crash onto the beaches.

As I sat there, I felt something shift inside. Instead of the sadness and heaviness that had been my companion for months, I began to feel something different.

I felt angry.

I was angry because, yet again, I had become consumed with a relationship. I'd fallen back into people-pleasing and

67

codependency. I was angry at how I'd allowed myself to be treated and how I treated him. Angry at the situation, the fucked-up-ness of it all.

This anger felt different, in a good way. It felt bold and empowering. I began to breathe heavier, deeper, as if I hadn't taken a breath in years. I pushed myself off the bench and began to walk, stalking the narrow cobblestone streets filled with happy locals and tourists, my insides smoldering.

Fuck this shit.

I couldn't do it one more second. I couldn't be with myself in this place, in this way. I had to move, to change, to do something.

That's the power of anger. It has the energy of movement. It is a gift if you use it correctly.

I went home, pulled out my laptop, and searched for flights to Vancouver. If I really meant it when I said I was going to be selfish this year, then it was time to prove it.

I found a one-way flight to Vancouver via Paris, where I'd have a layover for a few days. The flight left Valencia on Friday; it was Monday.

My heart pounded, and my finger hovered over the "Book Now" button. Was I really doing it? Could I? Did I have the guts? I closed my eyes and checked into that little place inside me where *Selfish* had come from. *Am I doing the right thing? I need a sign. I need to know. I'm terrified.*

Everything in me wanted to walk into the living room and tell Leo what I was thinking of doing. He was the one person I talked to about everything. But now, I could see that this was part of my problem. I'd abdicated my own opinion to his, in so many ways, that I didn't know how to make a decision on my own. I knew if I told him what I was thinking, he'd talk me out of it, and I'd be right back where I started.

Doorways 69

No. This had to be my choice. I had to take responsibility for my life, for my happiness, for my sanity.

I thought about my fantasies of going home, and the dreams I'd been having of walking through the rainforest. It seemed a lifetime away from the sunbaked streets of Spain. And yet here it was, only a click away.

I'd seen a post on Instagram the other day. It was a simple quote on a black background, and all it said was "This is the sign you've been looking for."

I thought about it now. I'd been looking for a sign to tell me that leaving was the right decision. Waiting for writing in the sky, or a voice from above to make it okay. But nothing ever came. Now, it was up to me. The sign I'd been looking for was how I felt, and what I longed for, and my dreams. That's all I had. Me.

My hands shook as I clicked on the "Book Now" button.

Ready or not, here I go.

Lesson: You are the sign you've been looking for. We can get so consumed with needing external validation to convince us we're making the right choice. Whether it's from a friend, our partner, or that woman on TikTok who always seems to say the right thing, that's never where the answer lies. Sure, we need guidance and expert support at times. But ultimately, the sign that tells you you're on the right track is you. Knowing and trusting yourself is the surest and wisest sign you'll ever find.

***

I wheeled my small suitcase to the front door that we'd picked out together at a warehouse outside of Valencia.

70 The Selfish Year

We'd combed the dusty aisles full of discarded Spanish doors, looking for the perfect one for our new home. Leo called me over from the far side of the warehouse.

"Look at this one," he'd said excitedly.

The door was incredible. Eight feet tall and arched at the top. The wood, while needing some TLC, looked promising.

"This is the one," he said. I agreed. I trusted his judgment when it came to renovating our apartment. He had an excellent eye for architecture and loved researching the best deals on each piece we selected.

The door loomed over me now as I stood in the entry. It looked solid and stable, a formidable barrier to the outside and a reassuring welcome into our home, the home I was about to leave with no idea when I would return.

That door represented a choice. I could stay on this side, in my comfort zone of the relationship and my home. I could stay inside of my hopes for our future together, stay in the appearance of a healthy, happy relationship, stay in the life I'd created with the man I'd vowed to love forever less than two years earlier. I could stay in the arms of a man I knew loved me and wanted to do anything for me. I could stay in the patterns and coping mechanisms I utilized to survive here. I could stay and try, for the thousandth time, to make it work.

Or I could open that door and walk into the unknown. I could walk into my fear of failure and disappointing others. I could walk into what I felt my intuition calling me to, without knowing how it would work out. I could walk into the pain and gut-wrenching sadness of leaving behind a life I had built without knowing when or if I would return.

Lesson: Discomfort is a portal; a doorway. It's beckoning you to step into the feeling and take action. When you do, your life changes, even if you can't see it at the time. Everything you want is on the other side of discomfort. Watch for those doorways and remember that life is giving you what you've been asking for. Then take a deep breath, and step through.

I had a one-way plane ticket in my pocket that, if I walked through that door, would take me to Paris for a week, then to Vancouver. No overthinking, just action, although I had enough presence of mind to know that having a return date would be a perfect opportunity to abandon myself once more and do what I thought I "should" do. I liked the open ending of a one-way ticket. I needed to give myself as much time as necessary to figure this out. It felt like the right choice, even though Hurt Girl was screaming at me that this was anything but right.

What do you think you're doing? This is stupid. Do you have any idea how many people are going to be disappointed, angry, and hurt by your actions? Stay. Swallow your opinions. Keep quiet. Do what you're told.

Her voice echoed in my mind and everything in me wanted to unpack my suitcase and keep the status quo. Instead, I kept my eyes fixed on the door and imagined myself returning in a month or two, rejuvenated, clear, stronger, and ready to finally make this work.

I'd decided that a week in Paris was a good way to kick off my Selfish Year. It certainly felt selfish to me, and the guilt over this indulgence followed me around like a shadow. I felt a little crazy as I'd booked the tickets and hotel. *Is this what a midlife crisis feels like?*

Standing there, shaking inside at the weight of what I was about to do, I felt myself begin to float above my body, hovering overhead like a ghost. It was as if, for a brief moment, I could see everything from outside myself. I saw my beautiful home; the neatly made bed, host of so many arguments, deep conversations, and quiet sex. I watched Lola sleeping in a sunbeam, safe and warm and sweet. I saw the French doors, flung open to the Spanish sun. I saw him standing in the kitchen watching me. Every one of my senses could pick up his mood, his energy, his emotions, like a finely tuned radar. I knew what lay beneath that inscrutable face. I felt the pain in his heart. Everything slowed down and I watched myself, about to walk out the door and blow up my life.

You are miserable, ungrateful, and self-centered. Look at you. You're an idiot, you're ridiculous, you're being dramatic. You are SELFISH. You don't know how good you have it. Why won't you stay and work harder? You are frivolous, irresponsible, and unrealistic. Get a grip.

I crashed back into my body with a thud, guilt gluing my feet to the tiles. I couldn't look over at him – my best friend, the one who knew my insides.

My plan didn't make any sense to him and I think he saw my act of booking a one-way ticket as a statement – a very loud, middle-finger statement.

I'd tried to explain that it was anything but that. I shared my Selfish word, and that I had to start learning to trust myself, and this was me doing that. We'd stood in our kitchen in the dark the night before, him on one side of the island, me on the other, and I tried to explain.

"We both know things have been bad," I said, my voice quiet in the dark.

"Yes," he acknowledged.

"I don't know how to fix this. God knows we've both tried."

"We've both given it one hundred percent," he said.

I knew what I was about to say needed to be said, but I didn't want to say it. I knew once I said the words I couldn't take them back.

"I can't be myself in this relationship right now, and while the idea of leaving is unbearable, the only thing harder is staying. I think if I stay I may not survive."

This wasn't an overdramatic statement. I'd had suicidal ideation more than once in our time together and more and more, I found my thoughts going to a dark place. I wasn't concerned that I'd act on it, but I was very concerned that I felt that the only way to escape the pain was to disappear.

I looked at his inscrutable face and felt frustrated. I'd called him a robot many times, trying to break through the disconnect I experienced. Not a kind thing to say – yet another desperate attempt to get my needs met through the wrong methods.

"I need some time to think, more than a weekend here or there." I watched his face, looking for a reason to stay.

"Okay. Whatever you need."

Part of me felt relieved that he wasn't making this hard for me, and part of me felt hurt that he wasn't fighting for me to stay. He left it up to me, and although I didn't know it at the time, it was exactly what I needed. No more looking for validation from someone else, being swayed by their needs or feelings. No more shape-shifting to please others. I was alone in this decision; I had to be.

74 THE SELFISH YEAR

Now here I was; it was real. The only question left to be answered: Would I walk through that door, or turn around and stay?

My phone buzzed; the taxi was here.

"I guess I'm leaving," I said.

"Okay," he said, not moving.

"Can I have a hug?" I asked, not feeling deserving but asking anyway.

He walked over and hugged me, and it felt like hugging a stranger. I searched his eyes for some signal that he wanted me to stay. I wished he would say something, anything to help me connect to his heart, his emotions. I wanted to feel wanted.

Instead, I grabbed my suitcase, opened the door, and walked to the elevator, wondering if he would chase after me, beg me to stay, promise to change. I heard the door close with a soft click behind me, and jabbed the elevator button to the lobby.

Waiting for the elevator to arrive, I felt my legs shaking and a rise of panic in my throat. Everything in me wanted to walk back through those doors and try one more time to make it all work. I could hear the elevator getting closer, slowly delivering my exit. I looked back at the door I'd just walked through, closed tightly, and wondered if he was standing on the other side, feeling the same way.

Seconds felt like hours; this moment became an eternity, waiting to be rescued by someone who didn't come. If he opened those doors and begged me to stay, I would have. But he didn't. Instead, the elevator doors opened, I walked through and pushed the button to the foyer.

I didn't know it then, but I would be forever grateful that Leo didn't walk through those doors and beg me to stay. Sometimes gifts feel like death when they're given to

Doorways 75

you, and it's not until much later that you can see them for what they really are.

Selfish Strategies

Change is hard. It's also inevitable. Regardless of how much we would like things to stay the same, nothing does. And yet as humans, we are wired to resist change, to stay where things are familiar. Our survival mechanism tells us that uncertainty is to be avoided at all costs.

The unknown is scary as hell, and it's inescapable. We can't predict the future; all we can do is take steps forward and trust that in the unfolding, we will be okay.

Our comfort zones keep us stuck in resisting change and maintaining the status quo, and if you don't know what your comfort zones are, you won't be able to get out of them.

A comfort zone isn't comfortable at all. It usually feels terrible. However, it's familiar. It's that groove in the record that your brain quickly falls into repeatedly. It's the well-traveled neural pathway. Change is so hard because of these pathways in our brains. We make the same choice and think the same thought so many times that it becomes a subconscious state.

If you want to create change in any area of your life, you will need to identify your comfort zones.

For me, the comfort zones I became stuck in during my time in Spain were a combination of thoughts, patterns, and actions. Thinking negative thoughts was definitely a comfort zone for me. I stayed in thought loops that focused on what was going wrong instead of seeing what was going well. People-pleasing had also become a huge comfort zone. It was the path of least resistance, the familiar terrible place

76 THE SELFISH YEAR

where I gave up what I wanted for what I thought someone else wanted. Regardless of what the other person really wanted, my subconscious decided for me, and I said and did things that not only went against my values, integrity, and intuition, but didn't get me the result I was hoping for.

Once I saw that I'd fallen back into those old comfort zones, I could start to move out of them.

So how do you figure out what your comfort zones are?

Pull out your journal, and let's do some digging. Ask yourself these questions:

- What do I keep doing, even though I know it's not working?
- When I'm triggered or upset, what thoughts do I have? Are they negative or critical about myself or others? Write them out.
- What emotions am I feeling when I'm upset? Sadness, anger, defeat, frustration? How often do I sit in these emotions? How long do they last? How hard is it to come back to a positive emotion?
- Where do I feel stuck? Where am I tolerating the status quo?
- What actions am I taking that keep me stuck?
- Where do I feel powerless to change my situation?
- What thoughts and/or feelings do I feel powerless to change?

The goal of this exercise is to identify the comfort zones you've been stuck in that you want to get out of. It might be patterns of communication in a relationship, or continuing to tolerate shitty behavior from a family member. It could be emotional eating or drinking that's damaging your health, or staying in a job you hate because you're scared to make a change. It might be feeling sad, or beating yourself up about everything, or comparison. Do your best to identify a few major comfort zones your brain has kept on a loop.

Now that you've got an idea of your comfort zones, I want you to consider how they're keeping you stuck in the status quo. Get real with yourself and dig below the surface. Write out everything you notice about how you're not showing up for yourself, keeping quiet, going with the flow, and operating on autopilot. What's the effect on you? How is this impacting your life? What's the cost of staying in this comfort zone? If you stay, where will you be in a year? Five years? Ten?

Next, it's decision time. It's one thing to want to get unstuck, and it's another actually to do it. It requires commitment. So again, you are going to take radical responsibility and, this time, commit to becoming uncomfortable on purpose and intentionally finding ways to put yourself in a place of discomfort because you know it's the only way to move toward what you want.

I, _____ know that discomfort is the key to growth, and I want to change and get out of this comfort zone that's kept me stuck living a smaller version of myself. I commit to the following actions that will feel uncomfortable but realistic, so that I will begin the process of change:

1. I will _____ by _____ (date).
2. I will _____ by _____ (date).
3. I will _____ by _____ (date).

Optional ninja power move: Accountability is a way to increase your odds of success. When you have someone hold you accountable, you are way more likely to implement. Find an accountability buddy! Tell them what you're committing to and by what date, and ask them to check in with you to make sure you've done it. Then do the same for them.

These exercises are designed to get you out of your comfort zone, which means you *want* to feel uncomfortable. I want you to stretch and challenge yourself but do so in a way that still feels realistic. Your nervous system won't like it and will begin to get activated, and your brain will tell you all sorts of reasons why this is a bad idea. Remind yourself that you are safe, that you are okay, and that you can do this. It takes time for your nervous system to begin to feel safe when you're stretching out of your comfort zone, which is why it's important to take small steps consistently so that you can settle into a new place before you move on. Be gentle with yourself, amp up your self-care, and ask for support when needed. You aren't trying to change everything all at once. Change happens in small increments. Let it be okay that you take baby steps into change.

The courage to change doesn't just magically drop in your lap. Courage is created by taking action. Each small step forward creates evidence that you can change. Every time you journal, ask yourself the hard questions, raise your awareness, and take small steps, you are building courage.

Courage is like a muscle. If you don't use it, you lose it. Just like going to the gym to build muscle requires consistency and persistence, so does building your courage muscle. You start from a place of fear. Fear of rocking the boat, getting uncomfortable, the unknown. It's all scary. You may not feel courageous right now, but I promise you are. You are brave and strong. How do I know? Because you're here, reading this book. That's all the evidence you need to know that you're brave. Trust that as you go through the process in this book, you will grow your courage muscle. As you do the work and implement small action steps, you will acquire more evidence that proves how brave you are. And one day very soon, you'll look back and be amazed at how far you've come and how much courage you've built. You'll see yourself showing up in new ways that you could never have imagined before. You'll feel differently. Act differently. You will start making decisions that reflect this. It's all inside of you.

The courage to change isn't something that you have to go looking for. It's right here, right now. As you uncover some things that have taught you fear and begin unlearning them, you will start remembering your courage. First Girl will start whispering in your ear and reminding you of when you were brave, bold, and didn't care what anyone else thought. She will guide you to your place of courage.

Client Story

Melinda felt terrified that one day she would end up broke and homeless.

Nothing in her life at the time indicated that this was a possibility. She had a good job working in human resources at a large technology company. She'd worked her way up to manager, had great benefits, and got a fat bonus every year.

And yet every time we met, all she wanted to talk about was the latest rumors of layoffs, her recent performance review (which was overwhelmingly positive, with a few growth areas), or the tanking economy. She lived in constant fear of getting fired or laid off. It kept her awake at night, worrying about how she would survive if she lost her job. With no partner in

(continued)

(continued)

her life, no kids, and aging parents, the fear of what might happen consumed her. In fact, it had gotten so bad that it was affecting her performance at work; her anxiety kept her second-guessing herself and hesitating to make decisions for fear of making mistakes.

The first thing we got curious about was her childhood. What happened to First Girl? When did she go into hiding? What made her feel as though it wasn't safe for her to have a voice?

Melinda remembered overhearing conversations her parents had about money when she was a young girl. Finances had been tight, and they lived paycheck to paycheck. There was just enough money for the basics, but not enough for extras. Melinda remembered feeling scared to ask for a new toy, or to take dance classes. Her First Girl had really wanted to be a dancer, and dreamed of taking ballet classes like her friends. But because her parents worried so much about money, she kept quiet. Hurt Girl showed up to keep Melinda safe. And how Hurt Girl did that was to make sure that she worried just as much as her parents. As long as Hurt Girl worried about money, Melinda would be okay. This began a strong subconscious program that would keep her in fear and scarcity for the next few decades.

As Melinda began to put the pieces together as to why she lived in constant fear of not having enough money, she started to see that it wasn't because there was something wrong with her. Quite the opposite. Hurt Girl had done a great job of trying to keep her safe. Now, as the adult, Melinda didn't need Hurt Girl to stand guard anymore. It was time to learn how to re-parent herself, so that First Girl could come out of the closet and, for the first time ever, begin to have a voice.

We worked with Melinda's self-talk, changing her subconscious thought patterns from fear and anxiety to safety and security. I also showed her how to regulate her nervous system. Whenever she thought about money, she would feel panicky in her body. This was a signal that her nervous system was disregulated, sending alarm bells throughout her body.

When this happened, I had her place her hands on her chest, apply a bit of pressure, and speak comforting and reassuring words to her Hurt Girl.

"I am safe."

"In this moment, I have everything I need."

As she worked with her brain and her body to create safety, miraculous moments began to happen.

She noticed a feeling of calm and peace wash over her body. She was able to be in the present and speak the truth to herself. Melinda's anxiety began to decrease, and she started to believe that no matter what happened, she would be okay. She was smart and capable, and she realized that she was really good at her job.

Melinda started speaking up more at work and feeling confident to make decisions. Instead of bringing anxiety to meetings, she began showing up with positivity and excitement. Her boss noticed and at the next performance review, told her she was getting a raise.

First Girl started showing up and speaking up. The very first thing she asked for was — can you guess?

Ballet lessons!

Melinda signed up for classes at her local community center, and for the first time in her life, she felt the joy and bliss of doing something just for fun. Every time she went to class, she thanked Hurt Girl for being so brave all these years, but she didn't have to worry anymore. Melinda the grown-up was taking care of things now, and everything was going to be just fine.

And she danced like a carefree little girl.

Chapter 5

Wandering

Chapter 5

Wandering

The next couple of months unfolded in ways I could never have predicted, and if I could have, I wouldn't have believed it. I'd left Valencia with no real plan except a few days in Paris and an Airbnb rental in Vancouver for a couple of nights. Getting on the plane was hard enough, let alone planning ahead. I'd never traveled without having everything booked in advance, right down to restaurant reservations. This time, I didn't want to play it safe. I needed the rug pulled out from under me, and the only one who could do that was me. So with a shaky grip, I grabbed that rug and yanked hard.

My feet landed in Paris, but my head was still in Spain. I couldn't believe what I was doing, yet here I was, doing it. Checking into my hotel in the 5th arrondissement, I still felt disembodied, like I had at the doorway to our apartment. It was like watching a movie of myself going through the motions: *unpack suitcase, hang up clothes, charge phone.* I got the sense that if I sank back into myself and really experienced this, I'd crawl into the soft bed, pull the fluffy duvet over my head, and never leave.

I'd been to Paris years ago, with husband number one and the kids, who were preteens at the time, and we'd hit all the tourist spots: Notre-Dame, the Eiffel Tower, chasing pigeons in the park, eating crepes and croissants. The boys fought in the middle of the Van Gogh room at the Louvre, and I made them sit on a bench until they got over it, laughing at the ridiculousness of it all. I remember vowing we'd go back again, just the two of us, and experience the romantic side of Paris. We never made it back.

This time I wandered the city in the frigid cold of late January, breath billowing above my green wool scarf, oblivious to the lure of the tourist spots. I had no interest in museums, churches, or towers stretching to the winter sky.

86 THE SELFISH YEAR

Instead, I bought flaky croissants and ate them while I walked, brushing pastry off my scarf and coat along the way. I ate in cafés, people-watching while I plowed through croque monsieur and rich red wine. The famous bookstore Shakespeare and Co. was a short walk from my hotel, and I went there every day, getting lost deep inside the warren of bookshelves, reading Jane Austen and Hunter S. Thompson. I went to the Bon Marché and marveled at the most beautiful department store I'd ever seen. It was like a chocolate box; everywhere I turned, something magnificent unfolded in front of me. The people were stunning, the displays incredible. Of course I couldn't afford anything, but that didn't matter; I felt so happy just being in the presence of so much luxury and beauty. It felt like a balm on my bruised soul. I breathed it in and wondered: Do I still have a pulse? Because I feel like the walking dead. Can beauty revive me? If it could, this would be the place. Lazarus coming out of the cave, but instead of rocks and strips of cloth, I had marble floors and Gucci purses.

I did buy something, a lovely handmade journal that turned out to be one of the things that saved me over the coming months. At the time, all I knew was that it was pretty and I imagined myself sitting in cafés writing deep thoughts. (In reality it looked more like sitting in my bed alone day after day, writing through tears.) That journal became my best friend, my lover, my savior, in ways I could never have imagined.

The days flew by, and I felt thankful for the distraction that Paris offered me. I was so busy drinking in the sights and sounds that I had little time to think about what I'd just done, and I felt happy for the break from the constant anxiety and rumination. On my last night, I had dinner at a small restaurant on a tiny side street. The maître' d led me to a table next to the window, handed me a menu, and gave me a wink as he filled my water glass. Dining alone had never bothered me, and this night was no different. I felt grateful to be there, watching people wander down the darkened street, cobblestones glistening from the recent rain. I devoured my salmon en papillote, then pulled out my new journal and wrote my thoughts. Afterward, I walked to the bookstore one last time, throwing my credit card down for Hemingway, Didion, and Fitzgerald, then wandered along the Left Bank underneath a clear sky sparkling with stars as a homeless man sat on a curb singing lustily in French. I passed under the twinkling lights strung across food stalls, suddenly feeling very alone in a city of millions. Entering the quiet streets of the 5th arrondissement, I pulled on my headphones and played the song that I'd listened to every day for the last few months: "Bird Set Free" by Sia.

This song had become a sort of anthem for me, a reminder that in spite of how dark and desperate I felt, there was a light inside of me, and I needed to find it again.

Back in Spain I had started walking every morning as a way to get some space and exercise at the same time. The Turia is an old riverbed that the city of Valencia drained and turned into a beautiful park encircling the city. It used to be the main access to the city for silk traders, who would leave their ships in the harbor and row boats up the river to the Lonja de la Seda, the beautiful Silk Exchange built in the 15th century. Leo would still be sleeping and I'd slip my shoes on, head out the door into the cool and quiet morning, take the stairs down into the park, and walk. I'd pass through gardens dripping with flowers, vast stretches of grassy soccer fields with boys and men kicking balls and shouting, and old men sitting on benches watching the action.

88   THE SELFISH YEAR

Each day after I finished my loop and began walking the few blocks back to the apartment, I played "Bird Set Free" and the tears came, as they always did, when I heard Sia sing about the scream inside that eats us alive. I wanted to scream to the skies, but I held it in, like Hurt Girl always did. Then the chorus started, reminding me that I have my own melody to sing, and to shout it out like a bird set free, and I'd let First Girl show up just for a moment, throw my hand in the air, and sing along.

That night in Paris, with "Bird Set Free" in my ears, I felt a surge of hope. I'd been numb for so long that it took me by surprise. I walked the dark streets shining under the stars, looked up to the bare trees and the black night sky, saw the moon in its fullness, and a tiny voice inside whispered, "You're going to be okay. Just keep walking."

And so I did. I kept walking forward, not knowing where I'd end up, but knowing that as long as I trusted myself, I'd get where I needed to be.

Lesson: When you're confused and lost, and you don't know what to do, just do one small thing. Focus on where to place your feet next. You don't need to know the whole picture, you don't need to know where you're going to end up. Just take one more step, then another. That's all you need to know. Stay in motion, even if it's a snail's pace. It's not a race. You can grow at a snail's pace! You get to decide how fast or slow you will move. The key is to keep making moves.

**

The Sunshine Coast is a beautiful area near Vancouver, British Columbia. A short ferry ride away and you're in the most magical place, surrounded by homes perched on rocky beaches, vast rainforests teeming with rivers, waterfalls, bears, and old-growth forest. I pulled into the driveway of the cabin I'd rented and my son Jordan and his girlfriend came running out to greet me.

Being back on the West Coast felt like coming home. A couple of summers when I was a teenager were spent on an island with my oldest sister, at a summer camp where she and her husband lived and worked. I took care of their young children while they were busy, but otherwise I was free to do as I pleased. I spent hours roaming the forest, sitting on the banks of rivers and oceans, daydreaming, and writing stories in a spiral notebook. I learned how to ride horses and would jump on my favorite pony and wander the trails. I always loved being alone, from the time I was small and would host tea parties in the trees behind my childhood home − one teacup for me, one for the fairies. Those teenage summers solidified my connection to nature as a place for healing and dreaming. If there is such a thing as soulmates, then mine is the forest and the ocean.

Our cabin looked out on the ocean and backed onto a huge forest full of walking trails. I looked around at the misty mountains, breathed in the salty air, and watched seagulls swoop close to the water searching for snacks, and whispered "thank you" to the Universe for getting me here.

I was exhausted, jet-lagged, and disconnected. We walked the trails, played games, cooked great meals, and sat by the fire. I slept a lot. Leo and I had talked very little since I left; he respected my space, and I took it. The pain I felt in my gut was a constant reminder of what I'd done, and talking with him just made it worse. I couldn't hear his voice without going into a dark hole, so for now, no contact was what I needed.

One afternoon, I sat with Jordan by the fire, the frothy ocean waves pounding outside the front window.

I struggled to know how much to share with him. I'd been very careful with what I'd said to the kids about their dad after our divorce. I wanted them to have the best relationship possible with him, and I never wanted to interfere with that. This time, though, I wondered where the line was between mother/kid boundaries, when the kids were now adults and my husband was their stepdad. I still wanted to be respectful of Leo and his privacy, and I didn't want to unload my problems onto them.

At that moment, I opened up a bit about the situation. Jordan expressed that he could handle it and wanted to be there for me. I shared some of my struggles and what had been going on.

"Mom," he said, leaning forward, "this is not good. It's not healthy."

"Well," I started, "it hasn't been great, but I hope we can fix it."

"This sounds like emotional abuse," he said.

I hesitated to agree with him, even though I had already decided that Leo and I were caught in some toxic behaviors, even though I'd said those words out loud before. I found myself defending Leo and denying the severity of the problems.

Minimizing is a common trait among people-pleasers and codependent relationships. I had a long history of minimizing my experiences and downplaying the reality of any situation. I defended and protected others more than myself and I glossed over the truth when it was hard to face.

As a recovering people-pleaser and former good girl, I fell back into this pattern far too easily. I worried about what my kids would think of me, or of Leo, if I told the truth. So I skipped over the details and painted a rosy picture.

After a while, though, the facade wore thin and I couldn't sustain it anymore. The opposite of a drama queen, I had become a faker, someone who wore a smile and said they were "fine!" while dying inside.

Telling the truth to my son at that moment was one of the first steps of coming out of denial. The fog I'd been living in cleared a tiny bit, and I heard that tiny voice inside me, and this time she said:

"What's been happening is not okay. It's time to see it for what it is."

I still didn't trust that voice, but I heard it a bit more clearly than before. I was listening.

Later that day I went for a walk along the beach, feeling the salt air against my cheeks and watching the surf roll onto the rocks. The rhythm of the waves soothed me and I took a deep breath, the first one I'd really noticed since walking out the door of my apartment in Valencia. I didn't know where I was going or what I would do, but I knew one thing for sure: It was time to speak the truth to myself – the brutal, whole truth – and this terrified me.

Lesson: If First Girl wasn't allowed to have emotions or opinions, or if she was overlooked or told to "stop crying," "stop being so dramatic," or other messages that she was too much, there's a good chance that your Hurt Girl became an expert at minimizing. In order to be loved and accepted, Hurt Girl had to exile that part of her that had needs or emotions, or needed attention. You learned how to gloss over your hurt, ignore unhealthy situations, and pretend everything is fine when it's not. This may seem noble or resilient, but it's really just a coping mechanism that keeps you in denial. Take time to stop and really look at what's happening, or how you feel. Journal about it. Sit with it. Get real. It's time to let First Girl have her say and be heard. It's time for you to acknowledge how you really feel. Come out of hiding and speak the truth, even if only to yourself.

***

Next I traveled to Edmonton, Alberta, where my friend Sam lived with her husband. My youngest son also lived there. He'd joined the military a couple of years prior and was stationed at the base there.

I knew nothing about the city except that it was cold. It was the beginning of February and I planned to stay for a month. I booked an apartment for a week, and had a second place lined up nearby for the next three weeks.

Being an empty nester still felt new, and it was weird not being a part of the kids' daily lives. I'd had a vision of what empty nesting would look like. I'd keep the big family home, and the kids would come for every holiday. We would have big noisy celebrations, there would be lots of visits, and I'd be the center of it all. I would be the sun, and the family would be the planets orbiting around the light, the home, the nest. That's how it had been when they were growing up, and I imagined that it would be like this forever.

Of course, it didn't turn out that way. Kids grow up and create their own solar systems, as they should, and we are left to figure out how to do life alone. It seems like we should know; we did it before we had kids, so what's the big deal? Except that once you've brought these humans into the world, you're forever changed, and pieces of your heart are out there walking around in the world without you.

I'd gotten the house in the divorce and, while it was beautiful, it was too big for one person. We had a lot of great memories there: long hot summers by the pool, barbecues with friends, birthday parties, and sleepovers. We also had a lot of painful memories there: their dad's escalated drinking, constant fighting as I tried to confront his behavior, manic episodes due to his bipolar disorder, and an ultimate descent into violence and chaos. Once I was single, I couldn't afford to live there, and as the kids grew up and spent more time away from home, the silent rooms haunted me.

When Leo and I decided to travel, I took the opportunity to sell the house and create a fresh start for everyone. At the time, it seemed like a great idea. What I hadn't anticipated was that while we were able to let go of some trauma by selling the house, we also lost the nucleus that kept our little family gathering together. Seeing the kids' friends going home to their parents' houses on holidays filled me with major mom guilt. Suddenly traveling the world wasn't as appealing, and every day I told myself I didn't do it "the right way." I'd screwed it all up.

Now, seeing my kids living independent, healthy, and happy lives, I felt a bit better about everything. While I knew that we had work to do to build our relationships as adults, I could also see that there can be a different way of doing things, and it doesn't change the reality that we are always family and always there for each other. It's okay for it to look different. Different doesn't have to mean wrong. That's not to say that they don't have their own struggles with their childhood, and with my choices. It's unavoidable. We are all doing the best we can with what we know at the time. When we know better, we do better. For me, a big part of doing better was to show up for my kids and give them the space and safety to express their feelings and share their experiences: of me, my parenting, and the past.

After my conversation with Jordan, I'd begun opening up to the truth about the state of my relationship. I knew that if I went back to Spain now, I'd fall right back into my old habits of people-pleasing and self-abandonment. I didn't feel strong enough to stay with myself when I was with him. However, everything in me wanted to go back: back to familiarity, back to my best friend, back to my comfort zone. It would have been so easy to book a flight and pick right back up. And yet my Selfish Experiment wouldn't let me. I had to acknowledge that going back wasn't what I really wanted; I had to admit the truth. When I listened in, *really* listened, I knew that I needed more time. I wanted more time.

Sam and I had some long talks, and she became a mirror for me, reflecting on where I had abandoned myself and showing me what I'd been unwilling to see. She encouraged me to continue being selfish and expressing what I needed. I took it to heart. I listened.

The first thing I heard my First Girl say was that I needed to tell Leo the truth about what I felt and what was next for me and for us. He'd been giving me space but I knew it wasn't right to keep going this way, even though I was terrified to put it in words. I felt nervous to talk over FaceTime; things always seemed to end in an argument anytime we'd spoken since I left, so I did what felt safest. I wrote an email.

Sitting at a café one afternoon, I opened my laptop and began to write. It wasn't until after I hit *send* that I realized it was Valentine's Day.

In the email, I explained what I saw were the major problems in our relationship and what I wanted and needed. I gave a deadline for seeing real change – six months. I figured that was plenty of time for us both to address the toxic ways we'd been showing up and to find better, healthier communication between us. I said I wanted to go to therapy together.

Then I said:

> "I need to do me for a while. I won't be coming back to Spain anytime soon. I'm taking it day by day, but the space has been good for me, and something tells me I need more time. I'm sorry. I know this is hard for you just as it is for me. All I can do is follow my intuition."

This was one of the hardest and most liberating things I'd done yet. For the first time, I'd shared my truth without trying to manipulate the outcome, anticipate his reaction or response, say what I thought he wanted to hear, or give him what I imagined he wanted. I felt scared at the uncertainty of the future.

Lesson: Saying what's true for you is a lifesaver. It doesn't have to be true for anyone else. It doesn't have to make sense to anyone else. It's your experience, and it's valid. Speak about it, and don't worry if the other person doesn't get it, receive it, or validate it. Detach from needing a certain type of response. The growth for you will be in the practice of speaking your truth. Talk about how you feel, what you want, and what you don't want. If the other person doesn't like it, reassure your First Girl, who is scared of not being heard. Talk to her. Let her know it's okay, that *you* hear her now.

> Lesson: Mom guilt sucks! We have so many expectations and ideas of what parenting is supposed to look like. A lot of it is based on comparison to other "perfect moms" who are "doing it right." It's all bullshit. Find your own way of parenting. The way that works for you will look different from everyone else's way because you are unique. Find what feels good for your family and be willing to create a way that may not look like the norm. Trust your intuition to let you know the path as your family evolves, and as you evolve. There are a million different ways to do family. Find your own way.

As my time in Edmonton ended, I still hadn't decided where I would go next. Sam and I sat on the couch in her apartment, catching up at the end of a workday for both of us.

"How long do you have this apartment for, Val?"

I took a sip of peppermint tea. "One more week."

"Okay," she said, eyeing me over her mug. "Where will you go?"

"No idea. But I'll know when I need to know."

I'd been telling myself this a lot. It reassured me that it would all work out and that it was okay not to have all the answers. I leaned into that belief, and even though a big part of me didn't trust it, I wanted it to be true.

I struggled to decide what to do next. Every time I tried to figure it out, my brain would close over the idea like water filling a hole and I couldn't make a decision to save my life.

I realized that I had never really made my own decisions. As a kid living at home, my parents told me what to do. As a young married woman, I relied on my husband to make all the decisions and followed along without asking myself what I thought about it. We'd moved 25 times in 24 years, and I blindly accepted each move, not asking myself if I wanted to go to Phoenix or Kansas City or Vancouver or wherever. I just went along with his ideas. When Leo and I got together, I relied on him to make decisions. He asked what I wanted, and I would align with what he wanted. It made life easy, I told myself. *Be agreeable, go with the flow*. I prided myself on how easygoing I was. I ignored the little voice inside that said I had an opinion.

So now, for the first time, I was on my own, and the decisions were only mine to make. My brain couldn't do it. The decision-making muscle had never been used, therefore it was as weak as a newborn kitten.

I knew that the only way a decision would get made would be if I looked somewhere other than my mind. I began to meditate, journal, and listen carefully to that small voice of my intuition.

I remembered how I'd always wanted to live in a cabin on an island. It had been a dream of mine for as long as I could remember, and I'd never done it. There had always been some great reason why I couldn't do it. Too busy, not enough money, too indulgent.

Why not now? It seemed like a selfish thing to do. Perfect.

I found a cute little cabin on Gabriola Island, one of the Gulf Islands in the Strait of Georgia, off the coast of Vancouver Island. I'd never been there before, but it looked beautiful and quiet. Exactly what I needed.

Booking the cabin, I felt a mix of excitement to have an entire month to myself for the first time in my life, and anxious about all that alone time. I also felt sad that I would be spending another month apart from Leo, and curious about what would happen.

It was around this time that I invented a new word. I'd come to see that there is a sweet spot of decision-making that really helps me. As I continued to make only selfish choices, I found a mixture of fear and excitement would bubble up when I considered a big decision; one that would get me out of my comfort zone in a big way, challenge me, and create an opportunity for massive growth, fun, and pleasure. This mix of emotions was the perfect recipe for moving me toward my best self, the highest version of me, my expansion.

I call it *terrixcited*. Terrified and excited, all mixed into one. That's how I felt getting on the plane from Edmonton, landing in Nanaimo, renting yet another car, and beginning the drive to the ferry that would take me to Gabriola Island. The winter sun hit my face, and I smelled the salty ocean air. Seagulls swooped overhead, and the dark swollen ocean roared to my right. I rolled down the window, stuck my arm into the cool air, felt the breeze lift my hand, and smiled the biggest smile since – I couldn't remember the last time I'd smiled spontaneously, simply feeling the joy of being alive in the moment. A feeling bubbled up that surprised me.

Freedom.

I pulled the rental car into the driveway of the cabin as the late winter sun hung low on the horizon, a dusky glow lingering on the dense forest that surrounded me. I walked down the driveway, taking it all in. The cabin had a wide front porch and a lawn sloping down to the road, and beyond that was a small bay, the water glassy and calm.

The silence stopped me in my tracks. I stood for a moment, stunned. I'd never heard so much ... *nothing* before. My breath whooshed inside my ears. In the distance, an eagle cried. The hairs on the back of my neck stood straight up, and I thought:

Here we go.

A couple of years ago, I'd been seeing a somatic therapist to deal with some of my unresolved trauma. It was an attempt to "fix" myself so that I could be a better partner. Although my motive was fucked up, the therapy really helped me to release a lot of trauma, and I loved the work. It's a very gentle process of allowing the body to show you where the trauma energy is, and then through a process of intuition, using memory and emotion, release the energy. The work changed me on many levels.

One night, in the middle of this time, I dreamed of a bald eagle. It soared above me and then slowly, gently, swooped down and landed in my lap. I sat in a field of wildflowers and stroked the snow-white feathers of this beautiful eagle, feeling calm, peaceful, and safe.

When I told my therapist about the dream, she helped me get curious about it. I had a strong feeling that the eagle symbolized a part of me, and as I stroked the eagle's feathers, I saw it as me, loving myself. The snow-white feathers represented my pure perfection. It became a powerful metaphor for my growth in self-love, and eagles became a special representation of the parts of me that needed care and attention.

So that day, in that silent moment, an eagle called out to me, and I remembered.

I remembered that loving myself meant getting rid of the rules that made me forget. All the rules that told me I should be selfless, that everything was my fault, that there was something wrong with me, that I was broken. All the rules that told me if I just did what I was told, what others wanted, if I did the "right" thing, the responsible thing, then life would work out. Loving myself meant that I had to make choices that other people might not understand, or approve of, or agree with. Loving myself meant booking a cabin on an island for a month even though it felt self-indulgent, reckless, and ridiculous. Loving myself meant going against everything in me that screamed, "Just go back to your life. Stop this silly experiment. You don't know what you're doing, and you're ruining everything. Go back."

In the silence, I listened to that small voice that I was still getting to know, didn't trust, and struggled to hear. I tuned out the rules and the "should" and dropped into a place somewhere inside that felt gentler, kinder, wiser.

The eagle.

I walked into the cabin, dropped my bag by the front door, and looked around. What hit me first was the smell: a mixture of musty cabin and woodsmoke that reminded me of every summer of my childhood. Jumping in lakes and camping in tents with my siblings while my dad and uncles sat by the fire watching for bears. Running through sprinklers and drying out on the crispy grass under a hot August sun. Orange popsicles dripping down my arm as my sister and I rode in the back of our station wagon with Lad, our collie. Ice cream buckets full of mom's chocolate chip cookies and lazy days spent reading Nancy Drew and listening to Abba.

Although it was winter, I felt transported to those childhood summers, and the tears came. I walked around the living room's old overstuffed sofa and brick fireplace, into the dining room with its wall of shelves stuffed with board games. The kitchen had a window looking into the forest, and the bedroom had doors that opened to a covered patio with a hot tub. I opened the doors and walked outside; the wind off the ocean hit my face, and the freshness took my breath away. To my right was a forest full of cedar trees and ferns. To my left, the sloping lawn with Adirondack chairs facing the sea. Straight ahead, the Pacific Ocean, roiling with whitecaps, waves hitting a small rocky beach.

Walking back inside, I felt a wave of guilt that I was here, in this beautiful place, all by myself. This was a home meant to be shared with family and friends, meals around the table, games played by the fire, late-night hot tub parties. And here I was, all alone.

Sinking into the old sofa and staring at the empty fireplace, I second-guessed everything. I felt stupid, ridiculous, embarrassed. *Who did I think I was, gallivanting around, throwing away good money just to sit here and stew about my problems? I should get a job, return to Spain, or find another therapist. I should suck it up, get over it, and make my marriage work. That won't happen sitting here alone.*

Everything in me wanted to grab my bag, drive to the airport, and book the next flight to Valencia. I imagined opening the big door to our apartment and surprising him; I'd run into his arms, and we'd have a Hollywood kiss. I'd change my ways; I'd stop complaining; I'd make it work. We'd live happily ever after.

One big problem with this idea was that I'd prepaid for the cabin. I'd gotten a great deal because it was the off-season, and the money was nonrefundable. Like it or not, I was stuck here for the next month.

While darkness fell, I marinated in my old friends Guilt and Shame. A quote from Deepak Chopra came to my mind, something I'd read somewhere about making mistakes. I pulled out my phone and googled it:

> "If you obsess over whether you are making the right decision, you are basically assuming that the Universe will reward you for one thing and punish you for another. The Universe has no fixed agenda. Once you make any decision, it works around that decision. There is no right or wrong, only a series of possibilities that shift with each thought, feeling and action that you experience."

I had to trust that this decision I'd made – not only to stay at the cabin but to be selfish for the year – would lead me where I needed to go. I decided to believe that there is no right or wrong choice and that the Universe would meet me in this decision and give me what I needed. I decided to jump in with both feet, trust the process, and see what would happen.

First things first: I signed up for an online course on emotional abuse. I decided that if it was true – what my kids had told me, what my intuition told me – then I'd better educate myself about it. I began to read, watch videos, and learn about emotional abuse – what it was, how to know if you're experiencing it, and what to do about it.

And boy, did I get educated. Almost immediately, I had confirmation after confirmation that this was precisely what I'd experienced. I learned about terms like stonewalling, gaslighting, silent treatment, love bombing, and isolation. I began to understand the effects of being in an emotionally abusive relationship: social withdrawal, low self-esteem, losing independence, shame, and loss of identity. For the first time, I began to feel validated, like maybe I wasn't crazy after all.

Along with taking the course, I began listening to podcasts about emotional abuse, narcissism, and other relationship dynamics. I started having realizations about my first marriage as well and the effects it had on me still, after all these years. I'd become an expert at compartmentalizing and shutting down, but now, with nothing but time and space, it all started to come to the surface.

I started journaling daily, writing down every memory, every thought, every feeling that came up. I wrote pages and pages, for once not censoring myself, letting it all out. Maybe it was because I was truly alone, and there was no risk that anyone else might find the journal and be horrified at the ugly words on the pages. Perhaps it was that for the first time in my life, I had no one to care for, to distract myself with. Whatever the reason, I quickly filled up my Paris journal and picked up another at the local drugstore.

One of the exercises in the course was to journal about anger. This one terrified me. I'd never truly tapped into my anger, and yet I knew there was a lot stuffed down inside; there had to be. I wasn't sure how to connect to it, and it scared me just to consider opening that door. As long as my anger was safely tucked away deep inside, I didn't have to feel it or deal with the consequences of what might happen if I unleashed the beast.

But in the safety of the cabin, I finally felt ready to go there. I decided to have an "Anger Day" and put it on the calendar to keep myself accountable.

The day came. *Anger Day*. I made coffee as usual, then walked into the living room and glanced at the journal on the coffee table, waiting for my rage. I built a fire in the fireplace to burn off the morning chill, laying paper, kindling, and logs, then touching a match and watching the flames lick at the edges of the paper, slowly turning into a small fire. Feeling the warmth, I sat on the floor, staring at the orange glow. I imagined it reaching into my core, igniting some tiny spark of anger that lay smoldering. I felt a heat rise inside, and I surrendered. I let the fire do its magic and grabbed my journal.

Sitting on the floor, I wrote pages and pages of angry words. I scribbled, wrote in all caps, swore, and said the ugliest things I would never say aloud. I wrote streams of words that made no sense. I wrote until my hand was cramped and the pages ran out.

Afterward, I felt as though I'd run an emotional marathon. Breathing heavily, sweaty from the now-raging fire, I laid the journal on the floor and became still. I checked inside – still breathing, still alive. It hadn't killed me. I ripped out the pages I'd just written and threw them in the fire, watching them turn black, burn, and turn to ash.

I felt purified, sanctified, holy.

Lesson: If it feels scary and exciting, there's magic there. Follow this as if your life depends on it. Get obsessed with looking for *terrixciting* opportunities. Experience what it's like to challenge yourself deep beyond your comfort zone and discover what you're made of. Get comfortable with being uncomfortable. When you see *terrixcited* as a clue, and you follow it along the path, guided by your intuition and a whole lot of gumption, you'll find yourself creating a life full of adventure, mystery, discovery, and growth.

***

I left Gabriola Island and entered a different world. During that month, the pandemic had been declared, and borders had begun shutting down. Being on a small island, I hadn't seen much of an impact. I'd rarely left the cabin except to get groceries, go hiking, and sit at the beach, so I wasn't aware of much beyond my little sanctuary.

My next stop was Victoria, the largest city on Vancouver Island. I still didn't know what the future held, and it seemed like a good stopping point to regroup and consider my options. I'd lived there ages ago when the kids were young, and it held many memories.

Leo and I had begun working remotely with Susan, a couples' therapist, and we were putting in all our efforts to see if we could repair our relationship and find a way forward. I knew a decision was looming about whether to return to Spain or stay in Canada longer. My intuition stayed silent on the topic (despite my best efforts to hear my "inner GPS"), so I booked a week in Victoria because I didn't know what else to do.

As I drove into the city, I turned on the radio and, for the first time, heard the news about COVID-19. I felt shocked and a little nervous about the situation and wondered if it would affect my ability to go back to Spain.

I pulled into a large condo building next to the Inner Harbor to check into my Airbnb and noticed the deserted streets and closed businesses. The city had a hush that I hadn't experienced before. The lack of cars on the road and pedestrians on the streets gave me a chill.

It soon became apparent that I couldn't travel to Spain even if I wanted to. There was no way to know how long the lockdown would last, but for the foreseeable future, Leo would be living in our apartment in Valencia, and I would be . . . somewhere else.

I felt pulled along in the unfolding of events, adrift in my little world of uncertainty, and now part of the global experience. Sitting in the condo at night, in a silent city, alone and untethered from every familiarity, comfort, and security, I leaned harder than ever on myself. I felt truly alone and scared at that moment, realizing that I had no one to help me, even if I wanted or needed help.

This began a deeper level of self-reliance than I could ever have imagined.

I didn't know what to do except look for a place to live that would allow me to stay as long as necessary until the lockdown lifted and I had more options.

I sensed that a more significant force guided me, and it wasn't just about me and my selfish journey. I felt that the Universe had me right where She wanted me: alone, adrift, and uncertain. Despite my anxiety about everything, I sensed a glimmer of faith and trust, and I kept returning to it when my mind screamed at me about why I should be panicked and stressed. The more I dipped into the well, the better I felt. I spent that week in a Ping-Pong match between my mind and my gut until I decided what to do next.

Lesson: When the shit hits the fan in your life, and everything in your mind tells you to panic, freak out, worry, and stress, go deep down inside. Drop out of your head and look for the glimmer underneath that is telling you something different. We all have a deeper place that holds our wisdom, connection, and guidance. Practice tuning out the voice of your mind and tuning into the glimmers. It's where you will find your peace, contentment, and reassurance that you will be okay and know what to do when you need to.

***

With trembling hands, I signed a one-year lease on an empty apartment in downtown Victoria. There weren't many options for monthly rentals, and nothing was furnished. I had chosen a small studio apartment on the ground floor of a new building in a quiet neighborhood lined with leafy trees. It felt like a good place to ride out the uncertainty of COVID-19 and my life; although tiny, it had a walk-out patio, and if I stood outside and looked to the right, I could see a patch of sky.

The landlord handed me the keys and left me alone with my small suitcase. The silence settled around me, and

I sat on the floor of the galley kitchen, looking around in disbelief. *What the hell am I doing? Am I crazy? How is this going to work?*

Tears came as the magnitude of my choices over the last three months sank in. I'd been so busy hopping from place to place, deep in crisis mode, that I hadn't stopped to let it all sink in. I'd been making choices from that selfish place, slowly building trust in my intuition, and the distraction of always having a new place to go had kept me from stopping to acknowledge what I'd done.

Now, on the floor in that empty apartment, it hit me. I had a home back in Spain. I had a life, a husband, a dog. This wasn't a home; it was a stopover on the way to . . . what, exactly? I couldn't see beyond the moment, and it felt terrifying. Again, I faced the idea that I'd never lived alone before and had always relied on a partner to help me make decisions. And again, I reminded myself this was precisely where I was meant to be, no matter how scary it felt.

I started to have doubts about the Selfish Experiment. It had begun to feel harder and scarier than I'd bargained for. I wondered whether I'd been kidding myself, and whether making decisions this way wasn't my intuition but delusion, narcissism, or stupidity. I craved comfort, familiarity, and my own bed, and I railed against the Universe, wanting to be anywhere but sitting on that empty floor.

After about an hour, I calmed down, remembered that there was no choice but to keep going, peeled myself off the floor, and got to work.

I'd kept my rental car for a couple of days to buy some basic things I would need. I went to Canadian Tire (for you non-Canucks, that's our version of Home Depot) and bought a folding lawn chair and a little camping table. I went to a dollar store and bought some basic household

108 THE SELFISH YEAR

stuff, then picked out some sheets, towels, and pillows – for a bed I didn't have.

Later that evening, I set up the lawn chair and camping table in the middle of the living room. I'd had the foresight to get Wi-Fi hooked up so I could work. I sat in the chair and looked around.

What the hell am I doing?

Lesson: When you're feeling stuck and can't see the way forward, and you are experiencing analysis paralysis, do this:

Take a deep breath. Stop and name your feelings. *I feel scared. I feel worried. I feel anxious.* Let yourself feel them. Find where they live in your body. Now, breathe. Witness yourself breathing. Feel the expansion of your chest, your belly. Remember that you are alive, and right here, right now, you are fully supported. Then ask yourself this question. *What's one thing I can do?* You don't need to know how it will turn out or what the outcome will be. Just do one thing. And after that, do one more thing. This is how we do it. This is how we find our path. We just focus on that one little step that will lead to another and another, and before you know it, you'll be somewhere totally different.

Selfish Strategies

We all have a subconscious set of rules that we live by. These rules were ingrained into our subconscious early in life, whether by parents, religion, school, government, or society. Your set of subconscious rules is unique to you. Because they are so subconscious, they are like your inner

GPS, determining your actions and choices without you necessarily being aware of the driving force behind them.

For you to start making choices from your intuition and power, you will need to identify these rules and begin to eradicate them. When I rented the cabin on Gabriola Island, I ditched one of my rules, which was "It's wrong to spend all that time/money on myself." Then I designed a new belief to replace the old rule. This is the new belief that worked for me:

> "It's safe to spend time/money on myself. I am prioritizing myself. I am caring for myself, and that's an amazing gift that will change my life."

Here's your opportunity to ditch the old, limiting, judgmental, fear-based rules that were imposed on you and create new empowering beliefs that will support your growth.

Journal time!

1. What are some of the rules I've been living by that limit me?
   - Rules from family
   - Rules from organizations (church, school, government)
   - Rules from friends
   - Rules from society (social media, movies, TV, books, etc.)
2. How have these rules limited my growth and kept me small?
3. What are some of the choices I've made in the past where I followed the rules? What was the outcome?
4. What are some new, empowering beliefs I'd like to adopt that feel better? (Tip: Take the old rules and play around with the opposite. For example, if one of your

110 THE SELFISH YEAR

old rules was "Good girls/women dress modestly," one of your new beliefs could be "I dress according to what feels good for me.")

5. What's possible for you if you ditch the old rules and start living from beliefs that are generated by your intuitive self? What choices would you make? What would you do differently?

6. How do you imagine it would feel to live without rules? How would it feel to live according to beliefs that you decide work for you?

Client Story

Anna struggled with the fear of losing money. She'd grown up in an immigrant family and was the first generation to be born in the US. Her parents came to the country with nothing and built businesses that supported her and her brother. Now, Anna, a highly successful corporate executive, lived in constant fear of not having enough. Although she made an excellent salary and had enough to support herself and give back to her parents, she felt crippled with fear that kept her from doing some of the things she longed to do, like travel, buying a home, and starting a family.

We uncovered a lot of subconscious rules Anna held around money, mostly from her upbringing, rules like "There's never enough," "Don't spend money you don't have," and "Live a frugal life and save in case something happens."

There's nothing inherently wrong with these rules unless they don't work for you. And for Anna, because these rules were fear-based, they kept her stuck in a small, unfulfilling life.

Once she saw that these rules were holding her back, she began to create new beliefs around money, beliefs like "It's

> *safe to spend money on things that are just for fun,"* and *"I am good with money, and there will always be enough."*
>
> *Then she started acting on these new beliefs. It took a lot of courage for her to step into a new relationship with money, but she did it. In small steps, she began to set herself free from the bondage of rules and experience the joy and freedom of her new beliefs.*
>
> *"Money doesn't control me anymore," Anna told me. "I control my money. It's just a tool that serves me, one that I can use however I want. I feel like I can breathe again!"*

Chapter 6

The Cave

I woke up in my apartment in Victoria and heard – nothing. The silence, so foreign to me after a lifetime of living with people, felt weird, as if suddenly my brain had more room, like I'd built an addition in there and increased the square footage.

I finally had a mattress. I'd purchased one that comes rolled up in a tube and then explodes into the most delicious, comfortable bed. My gratitude for a soft place to land at the end of the day was immense, and the irony was not lost on me. I'd left my lovely bed in Valencia – with 800-thread-count sheets, hotel-quality pillows, and a creamy duvet that felt like a cloud – to be here in a tiny empty apartment, crying tears of gratitude for a mail-order mattress, a camping chair, and a fold-out plastic table.

The pandemic was in full swing, and the silence in my apartment echoed through the streets. I found myself more alone than I'd bargained for, and even though my sister lived a few blocks away, my mom an hour away, and my kids a few hours away, we were all isolating, so the option to be with them wasn't there.

I had come to a strong belief that the Universe is always bringing us exactly what we need for our growth, and I couldn't help but see this as a cute little trick that, although wildly uncomfortable, provided what I'd been asking for in spades: space, silence, solitude, and self-reflection.

My dreams had been getting intense, and I filled my journal not only with my daily self-reflections and WTF moments but also with the dreams that stood out. Like this one:

> "I swam in the ocean, and when I walked onto the beach, hundreds of white shells attached to my skin. They were different sizes and would fall off like scales, but only when they were ready. Some stuck to my skin longer than others, but when they were ready, they would just fall off."

I trusted that as I shed the old, hard shells of my former self that no longer served me, more of my true self would be revealed. I felt beyond ready for a new skin, one that I felt comfortable in, that felt like the real me.

As the days passed, my journal became a place where I could understand what being selfish meant. In reality, it wasn't at all what I'd imagined. I had pictured myself being a badass at business, having tons of fun, and living my dreams. Instead, it looked like sitting with myself in a quiet room, watching the shells that had covered me my whole life, and waiting for them to fall off when they were ready, which wasn't as fast as I wanted, but always at the perfect time.

Journal entry, April 4:

"Protecting my energy has to be my number one priority. When I give energy to anxiety, fear, and distractions, I doubt my decisions. When I protect my energy, I feel empowered, purposeful, calm, and peaceful. I need to trust my intuition now more than ever. I am out on the edge of my comfort zone all the time. I am pulling away from the enmeshment, and it hurts, and it's hard. I feel the desire to go back into it. It fuels resentment and self-pity. I'm grieving the loss of my old identity, the "me" that others rely on, the "me" that got value from being needed. I'm now experiencing standing on my own. I will choose my happiness first. I will disappoint people. I feel like I'm betraying Leo; I'm married and just moved into my own place. I feel sad. I miss him. I also feel proud of myself for where I am now versus two months ago when I walked out the door. I had no idea on January 19, when I left Valencia, that on March 20, I would move into my own apartment. I surrendered to my intuition and the Universe, and every step unfolded before me without knowing what it would be. It's super scary to live this way, but it's brought me here.

I'm free. I had no idea when I bought this journal in Paris that these pages would fill with my freedom travels. My liberation. Freeing myself from all the ways I was chained. One by one, I am removing the chains, link by link.

Now that I am settled and I don't have to be planning my next move, the feelings will come — all the pain, heartache, sadness, exhaustion, and anger.

BRING IT ON."

Every day, I woke up, wrote in my journal, meditated, and walked. Some days I walked to the beach and sat on a rock, staring at the waves. On other days I'd walk through town or into parks and suburbs. I listened to music that matched my mood. Some days I'd tap into buried anger, resentment, and rage, and the playlist was moody and reflected my gloomy state. Some days I picked a happy playlist. Those were the days I felt hopeful and could connect to a glimmer of happiness. I didn't judge my emotions like I used to. Being selfish meant I allowed myself to feel whatever presented itself. While many days were spent in the pit of sadness, despair, fear, and worry, the fact that I wasn't stuffing or distracting my feelings felt like a victory.

My experiment carried on into the spring and early summer. I bought some furniture to make my place a little more comfortable. When the bed frame I'd ordered arrived, I eagerly opened the box and laid out all of the pieces. I'd picked out a cute headboard upholstered in gray fabric, and the frame had drawers in the bottom. I couldn't wait to stop sleeping on the floor. I pulled out the one screwdriver I'd borrowed from my sister; tiny and cute, it fit in the palm of my hand. What could go wrong?

Reading the instructions, I began to wonder what I'd gotten myself into. Tiny screws and parts covered the floor. The instructions didn't make sense.

I had never built any type of furniture before. Ever. I'd always had a man to do it for me. I was the cheerleader, the hander-of-tools, but never the builder. It had never occurred to me to try to build anything because I'd never had to.

118 THE SELFISH YEAR

Now, with no man in sight and no one I could call to help me, I had no choice but to build the damn thing myself. I sat on the floor, refusing to cry. Instead, I pulled out my phone and sent a picture of the situation to my son. In the midst of my pity party, I needed some support.

He replied, "You can do it, Mom! Just take one step at a time."

That was all I needed to shake myself out of the pit and get to work.

I quickly realized that the cute little screwdriver was not up for the task. Its short handle dug into my palm, and blisters formed within minutes. I also soon understood that while the drawers were a great idea, putting them together was a nightmare. I didn't have the strength to screw them together manually, so they were loosely held together, sad little drawers that worked but didn't exude any charisma.

It took me three days to build that goddamn bed. When I hoisted the mail-order mattress onto it and lay down, I felt like I'd won an Academy Award. I hadn't felt proud of myself in a long time, and lying in the bed I'd put together with my bare hands gave me a badly needed boost.

I'd showed up for myself and did something I'd never done before. I could feel myself growing over those three days, like a plant working its way out of the soil, and afterward I believed in myself just a tiny bit more than I had before.

> Lesson: Over time, we start to develop stories about what we can and can't do. We buy into the idea that we're not good at something, simply because we've never done it before, or haven't had to try. Like so many things, once you get past the story that's telling you a lie, you find out how capable you really are.

The borders opened and Leo made plans to relocate back to Canada. We weren't sure what to do with the apartment, but for now he would come to Victoria as soon as possible. He needed to find work, and our Spanish visas didn't allow us to get jobs there, so this seemed like the next right step. We were still seeing our therapist weekly, the three of us meeting on Zoom from our respective homes. As much as I needed space, I also didn't know how to move forward. I didn't want to initiate a divorce until I'd turned over every stone and explored every option to make it work, but now that I no longer denied the truth of what I needed in the relationship, I couldn't go back to the way it had been. I'd said the words *emotional abuse* and I couldn't take them back, nor did I want to. My eyes were wide open to the dynamic and how we'd both contributed to it, and so by going to therapy, I committed to working on my part, and waited to see if he would do the same.

I knew if anyone could help us, Susan could. She knew her stuff and didn't let us get away with our old patterns and habits of communicating. I began to see even more clearly why things had been so difficult for us as she started showing us the root issues. Our childhood traumas and coping mechanisms triggered each other, and when we were triggered, we reacted in opposite ways. I would need space; he would need closeness. It had become a cat-and-mouse game that left both of us feeling unsafe and hurt. We had our work cut out for us.

The Selfish Experiment was in full swing, and living alone drove me to seek a deeper connection to my intuition because I had no one to help me make decisions. I felt like a newborn calf struggling to walk on wobbly legs. Self-trust had been nonexistent, so flexing this new muscle had me doing a lot of searching and experimenting.

120 THE SELFISH YEAR

One of the most significant areas of growth was learning how to self-soothe. Previously, I'd always had someone to lean on and comfort me if I struggled. I had no idea how much I'd relied on that as a way to cope until it was gone. This hit home for me one day in the spring. It was a beautiful warm day, and I threw a book, blanket, and headphones in a backpack and headed to the nearby park. I found a perfect spot to sit and read by a water fountain surrounded by trees, flowers, and wild peacocks that roamed free. I read for an hour or so, then got up to go home. Stepping off the grassy lawn onto the street, I tripped on the curb and twisted my ankle, hitting the pavement hard. I sat there for a moment, feeling a sharp pain radiating up my shin. An elderly man approached and asked if I was alright.

"Yeah, I'm fine, thanks," I said through my face mask, unsure if that was true. I slowly stood up and tested my ankle. It hurt, but I was able to put my weight on it. As I hobbled the few blocks home, I began crying and hyperventilating. Not because my ankle hurt but because I had no one to comfort me. I cried because I was alone. I cried because I didn't know how to help myself at that moment.

When I got home, I put my foot up with an ice pack and calmed down, had a moment of clarity. Of course, I didn't know how to self-soothe. I never had to. So I would learn.

All of these experiences pushed me deeper into myself. If I was going to put myself first, I had to know who I really was, the "me" who lived underneath all my fear, doubt, and insecurity. I'd begun calling that place my "Inner Being." This represented the place that held my wisdom, that knew the answers. I'd been tuned into my brain and its survival mechanism for so long, thinking that would lead me to my

The Cave 121

best life, and it hadn't, so this Inner Being of mine needed to be the new decision-maker. She would run the show for my Selfish Year, which meant I had to hear what she was saying.

Operation Tune-in began. I started reading books, watching videos, and learning all I could about how to connect to my Inner Being. From my work over the years, I knew that our minds are not who we really are, although we've been conditioned to believe it, and that our true self lies in that place deeper down. You might call it the Spirit, Soul, Higher Self, or Intuition. Inner Being resonated with me because it spoke to that place inside that held the essence of First Girl. All my life, I'd been living from my mind; I used to call myself a "walking head." The result? Chaos, anxiety, fear, doubt, self-hate, judgment, worry, depression, sadness.

I'd dabbled in different methods of tuning in to my Inner Being previously. Meditation had been a sporadic practice. Meditation had been a sporadic practice, journaling and yoga helped, but my efforts had been halfhearted. Now my Selfish Experiment expanded to include finding practices that would help me connect to my Inner Being more powerfully. I needed to find access to this place within; it felt like my life depended on it.

I had already been journaling daily, which had become an essential ritual in my morning. Page after page filled with my experiences, thoughts, and feelings. Some days I poured out anger and rage; others, gratitude and happiness. Every day, I dug deeper and discovered new insights. I wrote down my fears, regrets, indecision, ideas, and dreams. Pen and paper transformed into an extension of myself that showed me more than I'd ever known existed.

122 THE SELFISH YEAR

After journaling in the morning, I would meditate. It started with 10 or 15 minutes of guided meditation and slowly grew into longer sessions. I began looking forward to this time as my ability to connect and sink deep expanded. My coach at the time had mailed me a beautiful journal, a pen, and some crystals. I didn't know a lot about crystals, but I felt curious and began researching the characteristics of the ones she'd sent me. I started holding them as I meditated, figuring it couldn't hurt. If anyone passed by my window those days, they'd see me cross-legged on my couch, crystals in my hands and on my knees, tears streaming down my face.

I'd found a YouTube video designed to create a deeper connection with the Inner Being. The woman in the video guided me with her soothing voice, and I visualized myself walking through a field of wildflowers, then opening a door in a tree and entering a large room. Inside the room was a table with two chairs. I would sit in one chair, and my Inner Being sat across from me. She always looked like a glowing outline, fiery and alive, with a slender golden cord connecting us. I would pour all my pain, hurt, disappointment, rage, and fear into the cord, and she would take it and explode it into fiery sparks that disappeared into the air. Then she would speak to me. Everything she said would make so much sense, and I would receive revelation after revelation. I found myself whispering, "Oh!" when I would learn something about myself because it all made so much sense, and the wisdom dropped into my being like a penny in a pond, sinking all the way to the deepest parts of me. Other times she would take me by the hand and we'd shoot into space, floating around with the stars and planets. She told me this was

The Cave

our home; this is where we belonged. I felt a deep peace and contentment during these times, and I felt safe and cared for.

I booked a session with an energy healer my coach referred me to. I'd never done anything like that before, and I felt curious and skeptical about it. A big part of my experiment involved opening to opportunity and going with what felt good, and when my coach told me about this healer, I heard an inner "yes." So I booked a call.

She lived in South Africa, so the session would be remote. We chatted on the phone, and she asked what I wanted to get from the experience.

"I'm not sure," I said. "I guess I'd like some clarity about what I'm supposed to do next. My relationship is up in the air. I'm living in limbo. I feel like I'm waiting for something, but I don't know what it is."

She sent me a playlist and told me to lie on my bed and listen for an hour. Meanwhile, she would be doing her thing, whatever that was.

I had nothing else going on those days, so lying down for an hour sounded great.

At the time of the session, I put on my headphones, turned on the playlist, and lay down. As the music filled my ears, I began to relax. I'd never heard music like this; it sounded ethereal, magical, with a thrumming in the background. I felt myself drift into a meditative state, and my surroundings disappeared. I don't know where I went, but it felt like I'd gone somewhere wholly safe, a place open to any possibility and beyond my physical limitations.

The timer pulled me back to the present, and I removed the headphones. She called me to tell me what she had been doing on her end.

124   THE SELFISH YEAR

"I sense that you are on a journey, that you've been lost, and you're finding your way home. You have ties to old relationships that need to be completed. You've been giving your energy away where it hasn't returned to you, and you're depleted. It's time for you to protect your energy and make yourself a priority. Trust yourself. You know what's right for you."

Listening to her, I smiled. It felt so good to have some validation for the path I'd chosen. Regardless of the outcome, I felt reassured that I was on the right track and had renewed motivation to continue finding my way back to myself.

Nature became a powerful way for me to connect with my Inner Being. I lived a short walk from the ocean, and every day I'd wander through the neighborhood, ending up at the coastline. A long flight of steps led down to a beach representing everything I loved about the West Coast: Huge driftwood logs, perfect for sitting on, stretched down the sandy shore. Shells and sea glass glimmered in the sun, and mountains loomed. I felt a magnetic pull to this wild and rugged place.

Sometimes I'd sit on a log and mirror my breath with the waves. A wave would come in; I'd exhale. It went out, I'd inhale. I imagined myself breathing in the energy, the life force of the Earth, with every breath. I always left feeling more connected to myself and to nature, more filled up and grounded.

The last thing I incorporated into Operation Tune-in was music. I curated a playlist of songs that helped me connect to my Inner Being. Some were moody and pulsating, others happy and uplifting, which helped me feel deep emotions and release. I'd walk the city, hand on my heart, singing to myself, feeling energy releasing. This daily ritual became something that I craved, and I always returned home with a new sense of connection.

The days slid off the calendar, and as the weather got warmer, I noticed a shift. The crushing anxiety about my uncertain future lessened; instead of waking with an immediate tightening in my chest, I would lie there and breathe for a few moments, feeling something else instead. A loosening of the vise, a release of pressure. I found a smile appearing on my face naturally, without having to force it. Those small moments in the morning, before I remembered where I was, or what was happening in the world, or what the hell I was going to do, felt like the most precious gift I'd ever been given.

The best part? It was a gift from me. All mine.

Lesson: Mornings are magical. It's an opportunity to decide how you'll enter the day, before anyone or anything else tells you otherwise. When you seize this window of time with intention, you're downloading valuable information into your mind and body. Before you pick up your phone, look at emails, or (please god, no) turn on the news, do this instead. Meditate for one minute. Tell yourself good, positive thoughts. Take a few deep, cleansing breaths. Remind yourself that you are safe, loved, and supported. This will change your day, I promise.

Selfish Strategies

Here are some ways to develop your own Operation Tune-in to help you connect to your Inner Being.

Deepen Your Journaling Practice

You've already been doing some journaling; now it's time to kick it up a notch. Your journal is your best friend when it comes to being selfish. It's where you can be completely honest with yourself and see your thoughts and feelings from a different perspective. I like to describe it as taking the "bowl of spaghetti" out of your mind and laying each noodle on the page. You get to know yourself in a different way. Commit to journaling every morning before you do anything else, before any external information enters your mind. You will be most connected to your subconscious, and you'll be amazed at what you discover.

A lot of my clients who've never had a journal practice before tell me they struggle with what to write. I encourage them to see it as a "stream of consciousness" – just start writing for a page or two and allow whatever's in your mind to come out through your pen. It doesn't have to make sense. If you don't know what to write about, write about that! Usually, after a couple of pages, you'll start to notice some deeper awareness and different thoughts and ideas will surface. Some of my deepest revelations and healing have come from this simple act. Commit to it, be consistent, and trust that as you do, you will create an opportunity for growth, healing, and a deeper connection with your Inner Being.

Challenge Yourself

Building my bed created a challenge I would never have chosen for myself if I'd had a man around to do it. And yet it became a symbol of my new independence and taught me that I am capable of so much more than I realize. What challenge can you give yourself that will get you out of your comfort zone, get you to try something you never imagined you'd do, and give you a dose of confidence and self-belief? You are capable of so much more than you realize and, honey, if I can do it, you sure as hell can! What's it going to be? Try a new sport? Put yourself on the dating apps? Book a solo trip? Pick something that feels just scary enough that you're peeing your pants a little but is still realistic. I call it the Goldilocks principle: not so scary that you will self-sabotage, not too easy so you don't grow, but just right!

Meditate

You have an Inner Being. You might have another name for it – Soul, Spirit, Intuition, Gut, Higher Self. Regardless, she's in there, living inside of you, and she's the source of all wisdom, inspiration, clarity, and power. She knows the way; she knows your purpose and destiny and how to get there. She's always speaking to you, just like your mind.

We've been conditioned to listen to the mind as our source for everything, and it doesn't work. I like to say that the mind is an excellent tool for figuring out what bus to take, but not for making life choices. Your mind has a strong protection mechanism that, when it feels threatened, kicks in to try and keep you safe. When you want to grow, it feels uncomfortable and scary, and your mind sees that as a threat to your safety. To grow, you will need to access the other voice: your Inner Being. You do this by turning down the volume of your mind and turning up the volume of your IB. You will never be able to get rid of the voice of your mind, but you can shift the focus.

Meditation builds your ability to shift your focus. It's like going to the gym for your brain. At first it's hard and you don't notice the results, but after consistent practice, you begin to develop those muscles and build strength. Find a practice that works for you; it doesn't have to be cross-legged with crystals on your knees. You can meditate by walking in silence, praying, chanting, being still, focusing on your breath. I suggest you use guided meditation to start with. It's like having a personal trainer. All you have to do is put on your headphones, press play, and listen. Try 10 minutes a day for a while until that begins to feel easy, then slowly increase. There are some great apps you can try that make it easy and fun. Some of my favorites are Headspace, Insight Timer, and Calm. I also love YouTube, where there are countless different types to choose from.

Process Your Emotions

If you're disconnected from your emotions, it will be challenging to hear your Inner Being because you'll be living in your mind, and that's not where she hangs out. Emotion is energy, and energy resides in the body. If you aren't processing your emotions, they get stuck inside of you, and you carry around that energy, which creates blocks to your Inner Being. It's like a river with a bunch of logs and boulders everywhere; they block the flow of water. Pull out the logs and boulders, and the water flows freely. Learn how to remove the blocks of emotional energy, and your connection to your Inner Being will be much easier. You may want to work with a therapist or coach if you have been carrying around emotions for a long time. Do what's necessary to begin to free yourself from the weight of your past. Be selfish about your healing. Your future depends on it.

Then grow in your ability to process emotion quickly so that you can recover back to a regulated state. Here's a basic process you can follow:

1. **Get still and drop into your body.** Observe what's going on. Do you notice tightness in your chest or a knot in your stomach? Be curious without judgment. Next, notice if there's a feeling attached to this sensation.

The Cave

2. **Name the feeling – out loud.** "I feel angry. I feel sad. I feel disappointed." Honor this emotion and give it space to exist.
3. **Feel the feeling.** Cry, journal, move, yell, dance, talk, listen to music, and do something that will help you to feel it. Most of us are good at "talking about our feelings," but that doesn't allow the feeling to pass through us; it keeps it stuck inside. Get used to "feeling your feelings."
4. **Recover.** Take a couple of deep belly breaths. Shake your body. Wrap yourself in a cozy blanket. Drink something warm, get a massage, go for a long walk, read a book, or listen to something inspiring. Give yourself a bit of time to return to a regulated state.

Stay Open and Curious

Once you begin connecting to your Inner Being, she's going to start giving you ideas, inspiration, and opportunities. This is when it's important to start trusting her. You've most likely spent many years trusting your mind or your Hurt Girl. Trusting your Inner Being takes time, and it starts with opening the connection, listening, and then acting on what you hear. It will seem weird at first, and what you hear will be a tiny whisper from your heart, your intuition, or your gut. You might start getting ideas about what you'd like to do, you might find yourself getting curious about things you'd never considered before, or you might start to get an urge to do something scary that you would never have considered before. Your fear is going to want to shut that shit down hard. Don't listen! Put fear in the back seat because your Inner Being is driving now.

I met with the healer in South Africa because the opportunity presented itself. I'd never done it before, and I felt curious. It turned out to be an incredible and affirming experience. Start taking action on those impulses!

Client Story

Jane was stuck in a cycle of self-doubt, fear, hurt, and sadness. Her husband of 15 years had had an affair and had recently disclosed this information to her. She felt crushed, defeated, and confused. He told her it was only once, that it would never happen again, and was working hard to regain her trust. Jane wanted to trust him again; she didn't want to lose the marriage. They had two teenage children, and she didn't want to put them through a divorce. And yet she couldn't "get over it." She suffered alone because she had no one to talk to. They didn't want anyone to find out. She also struggled with guilt and shame, feeling like she should leave him.

Jane had "lived by the rules" her whole life. She was the ultimate good girl and always put others before herself. A devoted wife, mother, daughter, and friend, she spent her days serving others without a thought for her own needs and wants. Now, her needs and wants wouldn't leave her alone, and she couldn't function anymore because she couldn't ignore her own experience.

I worked with Jane to get her out of her head and into her body so she could process her emotions. Then we worked on her good girl conditioning so she could let go of the subconscious programming that kept her abandoning herself. She got in touch with her Hurt Girl and began healing the old wounds from childhood. She reconnected to First Girl and started remembering who she was. Finally, she found her Inner Being, her Goddess, her place of power and wisdom. Once she began listening to her Inner Being, shit got real. She threw out the rules that had kept her suffering in silence and requested that her husband attend individual therapy to address his issues. They also began couples therapy. She began establishing healthy boundaries. She started taking care of herself, putting her needs first, and requiring that her children begin helping more at home. She started doing things that made her happy and excited her about the future. She returned to school, got certified as a yoga instructor, and started teaching classes at a local studio. She lost weight and got a makeover. She began building her confidence, independent of her husband.

Jane's radical transformation soon made an impact on her husband. He started realizing the damage he'd done to their relationship. He started to open up with her and share vulnerably and honestly. He worked hard to earn her trust back.

When Jane shifted from being a victim of her circumstances to getting her power back, she realized the truth: that when she is selfish, she gets happy, and when she gets happy, it doesn't matter what anyone else chooses. She is choosing her own experience, she's creating her own safety and security, and she is in the driver's seat of her life.

"I'm free. For the first time in my life, I'm free from feeling like I have to be someone I'm not for people to love me. I'm free from the rules. I'm free just to be me and do what makes me happy. I can let my husband make his own decisions. Whatever happens, I'll be fine because I'm fine inside."

Jane and her husband are still together and happier than ever.

Chapter 7

Haunted by the Past

ummer arrived, and so did Leo. We weren't ready to live together again; I needed space, and our communication hadn't improved. He rented a small apartment in town, a 10-minute walk from my place. I felt nervous to see him; it had been seven months, and we'd both been through a lot in that time. I still felt fragile and uncertain about everything, and although I missed him like crazy, I also needed my solitude. As long as he was in Spain, having space was easy. Now that he was down the road, I wondered how my Selfish Experiment would hold up. Would I be able to maintain my boundaries, or would I fall back into people-pleasing?

The day came to see each other. We'd planned for me to drop by and pick up a suitcase full of clothes he'd brought from Spain for me. I noticed that I felt more excited to get my clothes than to see him, and it made me curious how I would feel when we saw each other again for the first time in seven months.

Walking up to his apartment, I felt nervous. So much had happened since I'd left Spain in January. I thought back to the day I'd walked out of our apartment, fully intending to return in a few months. I felt like a different person now. I'd grown so much, and yet the idea of seeing him brought me right back to the doubt, insecurity, and confusion I'd been stuck in for so long.

I sat on a chair on the patio of his small apartment. He had to quarantine 10 days, so he sat inside and opened a window. We were only a few feet apart, but the distance seemed vast. My best friend, husband, and lover, the man I'd vowed to love till the day I died, looked into my eyes, and I felt numb and disconnected.

We chatted like old friends, catching up, discussing surface-level topics, and dancing around what neither of us was ready to say. The whole situation was stupid. I'd imagined something romantic or at least emotional. I'd pictured him shedding a tear and telling me how much he'd missed me, how hard it had been to be without me. How happy he was to see me. Hell, I'd even take a compliment. Instead, he seemed distant, detached, and withdrawn, like it didn't matter that we'd just spent seven months apart. Like I didn't matter. I sat there, dry-eyed, and realized I wasn't offering that to him either. I was just as complicit in this dynamic, and still I couldn't seem to cross the barrier that existed between us that felt as real as the window. I felt frozen, numb. A stone-cold statue uttering polite words and smiling.

I had to get out of there. I mumbled some excuse, grabbed my suitcase, and left, feeling more lost, confused, and alone than ever. Walking into my apartment (I had now lovingly named it "The Cave"), I grabbed my journal. I might have had old feelings creep in, but at least now I knew what to do about them.

The remainder of the summer threw me into a new set of challenges. The first half of the year had been an intense reckoning with myself, doing deep inner work, building self-trust, and getting clear on my issues. Now, Leo and I spent time together about once a week, working on connecting and bridging the gap our distance had created. We met for coffee or a walk, dinner out, or we'd hang out and watch a movie together. We were still in weekly therapy sessions. He'd made it clear that he wanted our relationship to work and that he'd do whatever was necessary to prove that.

I tried taking an observer's perspective when we were together: noticing myself with him, noticing him with me. I observed to see if I fell back into old habits. I knew it would be a true test of my growth if I could be honest with myself and him and not fall back into people-pleasing and abandoning.

One thing that we talked about a lot with each other and in therapy was intimacy. I had walls up, and I'd lost a lot of trust. I didn't feel ready to progress beyond friendship until it felt safer. Leo wanted to move faster than I felt comfortable with, and this became my first big test.

One day in therapy, he brought this up with Susan.

"She won't even hold my hand. We're married, and yet we act like distant acquaintances."

"Why is that?" she asked me.

I squirmed in my seat. Everything in me wanted to lie and give him what he wanted, but I knew I had to start telling the truth.

"I don't know, but I don't feel ready."

Susan leaned forward in her chair.

"It won't kill you to hold his hand."

This pissed me off. I knew what she said was true; of course, it wouldn't kill me. But I also felt that it was important not to betray this feeling I had inside.

The disappointment on Leo's face was like a knife twisting in my gut. I hated knowing I'd hurt him and was still hurting him, but now I was no longer willing to hurt myself to protect him.

I could feel something shifting inside. My First Girl felt safer because of all the work I'd been doing, and it became easier and easier for me to tune in and hear my truth. So one day, walking down the street together, I grabbed his hand to see how it felt. Surprised, he smiled and squeezed my hand. I paid attention to my body.

It felt familiar and awkward all at the same time. *Do I like this? Do I want this?* I felt conflicted. My body resisted the touch, yet my mind told me it was the right thing to do. I couldn't get down to the truth . . . not yet.

Summer turned to fall, and I had an experience confirming that the Selfish Experiment worked.

Our apartment in Valencia had been sitting empty since Leo left, and we needed to decide what we would do with it. I'd paid for it and all of the renovations with the money I'd made from selling the house after the divorce from husband number one, so the decision was largely up to me. Part of me wanted to hold on to it in case we went back. I suggested renting it, but every time we looked into it, the logistics seemed so overwhelming that we decided that wasn't the right choice. Holding on to it and keeping it empty wasn't possible financially, especially now that we were paying for two separate apartments in Victoria. I was bleeding money every month, and something had to give. In my heart, I knew I didn't want to move back to Spain; my chapter there was closed. Since I'd been back in Canada and closer to the kids, our relationships were getting stronger, and I'd been reminded that more than anything, more than any great apartment or amazing lifestyle, the most important thing to me was my family and I didn't want to create so much distance again. I knew it was time to sell the apartment.

We contacted a real estate agent in Valencia and settled on a price. He expressed his concerns about listing it during the pandemic, but we had no other choice.

This threw me into a lot of grieving. Buying, renovating, and decorating our home had been an incredible experience. I only got to live in it for three months, and because that time had been so stressful, I didn't get to enjoy it in the way I'd wanted. When I left, I had no idea that I would never return. At the time, I imagined being gone for a couple of months at the most. My Selfish Experiment had led me in directions that I'd never anticipated, and if you'd told me in January that I'd be sitting in an apartment in Victoria in September, I would have laughed in your face.

I let myself process the grief, anger, sadness, and loss. I hired a photographer to take pictures of the apartment, and when she emailed them to me, I spent hours staring at the images and imagining what could have been. The gleaming copper tub, the wooden shutters we'd refinished that opened onto the small balconies overlooking the street. I remembered standing on the balcony on Christmas Eve, listening to church bells ringing all over the city, feeling like the luckiest girl in the world.

Eventually, I returned to a place of calm and acceptance. I let it go and trusted, once again, that this was the right decision because my intuition told me. I released my beloved home to the Universe and knew that whatever happened, everything would work out.

Walking home one night after dinner with Leo, listening to my playlist and feeling particularly open and connected, I had a little chat with the Universe.

"I want a spiritual experience," I whispered into the black night sky. "I want you to show me that you're real and that we really are co-creating this life together. I'm ready."

Later that night, I woke up with an intense feeling of anxiety and worry. I lay there thinking about the apartment, wondering when it would sell, doing numbers in my head to figure out how long I could continue to pay the mortgage. Aware that this was a slippery slope to go down at three in the morning, I tried to shut my brain off and go back to sleep but felt wide awake. I decided to meditate to calm my mind, so I sat up, crossed my legs, closed my eyes, and began to breathe. For a few minutes, my mind raced,

140   THE SELFISH YEAR

but as I focused on my breath, a calm enveloped me. Soon,
I felt a deep peace through my body, and my breathing
slowed even more.

What happened next is what I can only describe as a
vision. I saw the apartment in Spain, glowing in the sunlight,
and two men walking around. I didn't recognize either of
them, but I knew instinctively that one of them was our
real estate agent (we had only talked via email and phone).
The other man walked through the place with a smile and
said that he loved it. He said that he could see himself living here and that he knew this was meant to be his home.

I felt a deep calm and peace fill my body, and as the
vision faded, I knew beyond doubt that the apartment
would sell to the perfect person, at the perfect time, for
the perfect price. I snuggled under my blankets and fell
back to sleep.

The next morning, I woke with a sense of excitement
about my vision. I wanted to call Leo and tell him about it.
Picking up my phone, I noticed he'd already sent me a text.
It said, "The agent emailed me this morning. He showed
the apartment to someone, and they want to make an offer."

Chills ran through my body, and I felt a thrill. Could
it possibly be that my vision was a reflection of reality? I
told him to ask our agent when he'd shown the apartment.
It turned out that he'd taken a man through at 11:00 a.m.,
which, with the time difference, was 2:00 a.m. for me, one
hour before my vision.

Later that day, we received an offer that was less than
we hoped to get. Leo and I discussed it and, while it was
tempting just to accept it, we both felt that we wanted to
counter with a price closer to what we'd been asking. We
sent it to the agent and waited.

Haunted by the Past

He called us shortly after and said, "The buyer fell in love with your apartment. He wants it, and he wants all of your furniture as well. Before I could present your counter, he removed his original offer and submitted a new offer. It's for the exact price of your counter."

The night before, when I'd asked the Universe for a spiritual experience, I had no idea what, if anything, would happen. I'd been shown in no uncertain terms that all the work I'd been doing was paying off. I knew I was going in the right direction and that the Selfish Experiment was becoming a certainty. The deeper I connected to my Inner Being, the more I heard her voice and the more I acted on it, the stronger my connection to the Universe. This co-creation, the mingling of our energies, made shit happen. Putting myself, my needs, my desires, and my connection to myself first had set me on a path of synchronicities, opportunity, possibility, and magic. I felt more resolute than ever that I didn't need to know the outcome; all I needed to know was the next right step, and that step would be made clear to me when I did the work to stay connected.

My Inner Being was a fucking Goddess.

Autumn brought crisp, bright mornings, warm days, and a realization that my Selfish Year would soon be over. I'd settled into the routines that connected me to my Inner Being; they'd become my lifeline, my one constant in a sea of change. However, after the excitement of selling the apartment and the high of seeing my vision become a reality, I fell into a funk that lasted for days. I'd grown tired of the constant uncertainty of my life, and my resolution to break old patterns and habits grew thin. I began spending more time with Leo, and we'd fallen back into our pattern of talking for hours and analyzing each other, ourselves, and our relationship. It gave me something to hold on to, and

142 THE SELFISH YEAR

although it irritated me most of the time, I felt like a moth to a flame, unable to resist the draw of the old, familiar patterns. He continued to express his love for me and desire to make things work, and I have to admit, it felt damn good to hear. Also, after so many months alone, it was nice to have someone to sit next to on the couch watching movies.

Lesson: Comfort zones are sneaky. Our minds and bodies cling to the familiar because, even if our logical mind tells us that person or thing isn't good for us, on some level it feels safe. We can very easily find ourselves gravitating back to old habits. We must be diligent when creating change in our lives. Resist the pull of the familiar, lean into the discomfort of the new, and remind yourself that even though everything inside you is screaming at you to go back to old familiar shores, you will keep your eye on the new land ahead.

Having a continent and an ocean between us had made it easier for me to cultivate meeting my own needs instead of disappearing inside the relationship. Now that only a few blocks separated us, I kept hoping for a sign that we'd grown and unlearned our trauma patterns and ways of communicating enough to forge a healthy future together. Every conversation, every moment we spent together, I hoped and prayed for my Inner Being to say:

"Here it is. This is what you've been longing for. It's here; you are safe inside this relationship."

Instead, I became increasingly aware that we were showing up in the same ways. We now had a greater awareness of *why*, but still seemed unable to offer each other emotional safety and rebuild trust. My deeper connection to my intuition gave me an awareness I couldn't ignore. I felt our relationship slipping away, yet I couldn't let go.

Something else I couldn't ignore was the anger lurking deep inside me, like a tiger waiting for its prey. Yes, I'd had my Anger Day back at the cabin. Yes, I'd processed a lot of repressed anger. *Isn't that enough? Can't it be a one-and-done type of deal?* The people-pleaser part of me would never allow myself to feel anger, let alone express it. Now I found an outlet in my journal and started letting it out in the safety of the pages. It felt scary to acknowledge how angry I felt, and yet I had to get it out, or the tiger would consume me as its prey.

Here's a page from my journal:

"I'm so fucking angry. I don't trust him. I don't know if I love him. I feel so hurt, abandoned, and fucking pissed. I'm furious. Therapy sucks because I don't say what I really mean. The truth is, I don't want to connect. I don't want to open my heart again. I don't give a goddamn about his feelings. Am I ready to end it? What's keeping me here? What's left that's good? I'm exhausted. Therapy is bullshit. It's all "look into each other's eyes and notice what you love about each other," and all I can think and feel is rage. I'm so over it; I'm done being nice; I don't want to be open and connected. I don't care anymore."

The next day, I sat on the couch in my Cave with a bottle of wine and turned on the one movie I knew could connect me deeper to my feelings than anything else. *Eat Pray Love* had become my touchstone over the years. (Yup, the same movie I'd watched with Leo on the couch years ago, and ignored my Inner GPS. The Universe loves a good joke.) I'd read the book by Elizabeth Gilbert at one of my darkest times, when I was at the end of my first marriage, feeling lost, alone, and terrified. Reading about her solo journey through Italy, India, and Bali after leaving her marriage infused me with so much hope and inspiration. It sparked a tiny glimmer of courage within me that maybe I, too, could advocate so fiercely for my freedom that I could take a journey home, whether through travel or simply within myself. I turned on the movie and waited for the moment I knew would wreck me: the scene where Julia Roberts, as Liz, arrives in Rome and the camera pans over the Italian rooftops. The music swells, and she starts her journey of healing and coming home to herself.

Immediately, I transported back two years earlier to the month Leo and I lived in Rome, amid the same rooftops, feeling the magic, freedom, and possibility. I saw our little apartment, a few blocks from the Spanish Steps, like it was yesterday. We'd decided to elope because it felt exciting, fun, and free. I'd felt sad that my kids wouldn't be there and wondered if I was doing the right thing, but I went for it anyway.

We'd planned a dream wedding. I found a dress in Canada only a week before we got on the plane. I had planned to buy a simple cocktail dress, but when Victoria and I went to the bridal shop, I tried on a traditional long wedding gown. Looking at myself in the mirror, I felt sexy, glamorous, and *molto benne*. I carried it in my suitcase during our month living in Florence, then to our little apartment in Rome, and every now and then would try it on to make sure all the pasta and bread and wine hadn't busted me out of the fitted bodice.

The day of our wedding, the hair stylist and makeup artist arrived at our apartment to get me ready. My bouquet arrived, scenting the room with lilies. I slipped on my

Haunted by the Past 145

dress and the photographer got ready to shoot "the reveal."
I stood, self-conscious, in the tiny living room where Leo
stood with his back to me, wearing the wedding suit we'd
picked out at a boutique in the city. He turned around, and
I waited for emotion to cross his face, but I didn't see anything. He smiled, and we embraced. I felt disappointed and
wondered if I'd set my expectations too high by watching
videos of other grooms seeing their bride for the first time,
crying tears of emotion, but I pushed the feelings away and
moved on. The driver waited in the tiny cobblestone alley
to take us to the Campidoglio for the ceremony.

Bustling out into the street, the driver smiled and waved
from the vintage car we'd rented. He drove us through the
Roman streets in late afternoon, and as we cruised past the
Colosseum and the Forum, locals waved and shouted "Agurri!"
("Congratulations!"). We walked into the Campidoglio, both
of us feeling the weight of history in every step. The room was
small but, in typical Italian style, every inch was decorated in
gold plating, dark red velvet, and frescoed ceilings. We stood
for the Italian ceremony, and although we didn't have a clue
what the guy said, we didn't care, and we held tightly to each
other's hands.

Then we said our vows to each other. Writing my vows
had come easily, and I said them with a shaking voice and
tears, our eyes locked on each other.

"Today and every day from now forward, I choose you. I have
the word 'choice' tattooed on my wrist because I realized, years
ago, that I always have a choice, even if it's choosing a different
perspective or thought. And the word has served me well. Today,
I give that word to you. I choose you; When life gets hard, I will
choose to love you. When I don't feel like it, I will still choose
you. When I'm afraid to open my heart, I will choose to offer it
to you because I trust you. My heart is at home with you."

146   THE SELFISH YEAR

After the ceremony, we walked to a large stone patio overlooking the Forum. Standing in front of one of the most ancient cities, I looked at him with shining eyes and felt like the luckiest girl in the world.

The romance of the day made it easy to forget that only the week before, we'd walked through the same city as golden hour faded to night, yelling at each other for two hours.

"Why can't you just listen to me?" I'd shouted, ignoring the tourists milling around us. "Why does everything have to be an exhausting analysis? Why can't you let me have my feelings without telling me I'm wrong to have them?"

"I'm letting you have your feelings. You just don't see it," he'd replied. This made me see red and I thought, maybe if I just say it in a different way, one more time, he'll understand me.

Exhausted, we walked back to our apartment and he poured me a glass of wine in silence. I drank it in the dark, wondering if I should cancel the wedding, then, thinking about all the nonrefundable deposits, went to bed instead.

I turned off *Eat Pray Love* at the part when she leaves Italy and heads for India. I didn't need to see the rest. I took a shaky breath, finished the glass of wine, and sat in the quiet stillness of my dark apartment. Touching the wedding ring Leo gave me on a trip to Costa Rica, I watched the diamond glimmer in the dark. Would I break the vows I'd said that day in Rome? Was I willing to go back on my word? Did I have good enough reasons? Neither of us had cheated, and when things were good between us, they were amazing. But the good had diminished to about 10% of the time, and the other 90% was so hard. I'm a loyal person: When I commit, I will do everything in my power to make it work. I'd stayed in my first marriage about 10 years too long because I kept trying. Now I considered the idea

Haunted by the Past

of leaving, and it felt like my personal mission to keep my vows and to make it work.

And yet, this year taught me that when I choose myself first, everything works out. Maybe it was time to make some vows to myself. Maybe it was time to take the word I'd written on my wrist – *choice* – and make it mean something else.

I'd been choosing myself for 10 months, and now it was time to go to the next level. To choose myself even when I didn't want to, when everything inside resisted being selfish. When all of my conditioning, programming, and hurt told me to go back to what felt safe and familiar. Hurt Girl began showing up, acting out, and wanting attention. Even considering leaving my marriage created chaos within, because she didn't feel safe with just me. I hadn't cultivated enough inner safety to help her relax, heal, and allow me to move into a terrifyingly unknown future.

It was never or now. I would either continue to self-soothe in destructive ways, or I would give her what she'd always needed: safety, not from any person or external thing, but safety from me. The adult me, the only one who could give her what she didn't get as a child.

Journal entry:

"My Hurt Girl is afraid, but I'm helping her feel safe. At the beach . . . she loves picking shells, walking, and sitting on a log watching the waves. She's scared and it's okay. I brought two men into her life who she didn't feel safe with. I will create safety for her now. She needs me to protect her. She needs to know I will stand up and fight for her, not abandon her. My choices have scared her, so it will take time to rebuild trust.

A foghorn is sounding through the mist, an ancient warning to beware, avoid the rocks, avoid destruction. I've been ignoring the foghorn inside of me that's always been there, warning me of danger. I've ignored it by numbing out, distracting, and avoiding. I have done that with food, alcohol, media, shopping, men. If I distracted myself, I didn't have to hear the danger signal, and then I wouldn't have to make scary choices. I could just let the current carry me. I veered into destruction so many times. When I listen and pay attention, I can navigate around the rocks and get to my destination: love, joy, connection, peace, abundance. I'm so grateful for my Hurt Girl. Today she needs peace, quiet, good food, and exercise. I will give her that. When she feels safe, it allows First Girl to surface, and she's the one who contains all of my excitement, creativity, passion, and ambition. She's the force of nature who always existed inside. She's making more of an appearance these days, and it's amazing."

Amid the turmoil of our relationship, I began feeling new excitement about my business. I'd been on cruise control for most of 2020, maintaining my private clients but not pushing into new growth. I'd barely had the energy to exist, and I hadn't felt creative or inspired in ages. The energy and focus I'd been pouring into trying to save the marriage had consumed me, and besides that, my healing and Selfish Experiment took most of my time outside of client calls. Now I began to wonder what kind of energy would be released if I stopped pouring it into my relationship. What would be possible? I found myself experiencing a growing excitement about new directions and began dusting off some of my old dreams and goals that had gotten shoved on a shelf when life descended into chaos.

Survival mode sucks. It's that place where all you can do is the basics. There's no energy for creating anything new because all you've got is enough energy to keep going from day to day. I'd been there before, many times, and here I was again. Same train, same station. Nowheres-ville. I felt so over it and ready to hop on a different train and go somewhere new.

One of my dreams that I'd had for years was to be a public speaker. I could see myself on a stage, speaking to thousands of people, inspiring them, sharing my heart, making an impact, and changing lives. It had been on the "Someday Shelf" for so long – that shelf where we put our dreams when they are too big and scary to do anything about, so they just sit there, getting dusty. Once in a while we see it out of the corner of our eye and think, "Oh yeah! Someday, I'll get to that. Someday, I'll go for that dream. But not now. Now is not the time." The Someday Shelf is where we stick our dreams because we know, deep down, that if we were to grab hold of it, we would have to require more of ourselves. We'd have to actually work on growth, and become a bigger version of ourselves. And that's scary as hell, so no thank you! Stick it up on the Someday Shelf and I can tell myself that I still have a dream, and as long as it's up there, I don't feel like I've entirely given up, but I don't have to do anything about it. Super safe. Super comfy. Super boring.

My dream of speaking and having a bigger message to reach more people had been up there for so long it felt like a distant memory, something that sounded good but never required me to do anything about it. And yet I'd been noticing it more. I peeked up at my Someday Shelf more often, and started feeling some excitement about this possibility. I couldn't see what that would look like yet, had no idea how it would happen, but I felt something rising within me that kept me intrigued. I began taking that dream down and blowing off the dust. I began imagining myself on a stage. I began feeling the excitement of the possibility.

At the same time, my isolation and hours spent in my Cave were the complete opposite of this dream, and it seemed impossible. One afternoon, I made a cup of peppermint tea, curled up on my couch, and wrote about this.

150 THE SELFISH YEAR

Page after page poured out of me about this dream I'd had my entire life and that I'd always kept on the Someday Shelf because I never believed it could happen. Now, though, I knew that if I had a dream, it's because it was meant for me, and it wasn't because the Universe wanted to play a cruel joke. I also knew it was up to me to do my part in moving toward it and stepping into the fear of the bigness of my dream.

As I wrote, a memory surfaced that caught me off guard, something I hadn't thought about in years.

Fifteen years ago, my dad was dying. He'd been diagnosed with lung cancer only a few months earlier, and although he'd been sick for years with other complications, he began a rapid descent to the end of his life. My mom let us kids know and we all arrived at the hospital to say our goodbyes.

My relationship with my dad was complicated. It had been great when I was little. He was funny, always making me laugh, and intelligent, challenging me to think about things in new ways. He was the director of the museum in our town, and I spent many weekends there after hours while he worked, sitting among the mounted animals, imagining conversations and adventures with them. I'd write stories about the snow leopard, the deer, and the black bear. My favorite was the grizzly bear, standing on hind legs, looming tall over my tiny five-year-old self. He both terrified and excited me; that's where my first experience with *terrixcited* (my made-up word I mentioned back in Chapter 5) began. I sat under his huge paws, experiencing a sense of safety there. The local paper even took photographs of me sitting under the grizzly and among the other animals for a feature story about the museum. I sat on the ground, cross-legged, my hair pulled into two pigtails, wearing my favorite Mickey Mouse jumpsuit. I patted the deer's head as the photographer took the photos, until finally I turned to my dad and said, "My patting muscles are getting tired."

First Girl had a great time with my dad. One of my favorite photos is of us walking down a road holding hands. I'm captured mid-skip, arms akimbo, mouth open in a gleeful and free howl of pleasure.

Then there was the other dad. The one who, when I was eight, took me into his dark bedroom in the middle of the afternoon and molested me. The one who became a predator in my own home, the one who I began to see as dangerous. It happened a few times, and then, one day, something rose up in me, and I just refused to do what he asked. I said no, and I meant it. My eight-year-old self wasn't having it.

After that, he never touched me again, but the damage was done. Hurt Girl took over and began weaving a life of fear and self-protection. The goofy, crazy, daydreaming kid who played with the animals in her imagination disappeared, and the responsible, good, wary, angry girl took over.

I'd done a lot of therapy by the time I stood at my dad's bedside, watching him die. I'd confronted him about the abuse and set strong boundaries. He'd never gotten help and so I had minimal contact. I no longer felt angry, or even hurt. I was able to stand there with love, feel the loss and devastation his pain had wreaked on my family, and hold it all at the same time.

We said our goodbyes. He was in and out of lucidity, but I could tell he was aware that we were there, and for the first time in my life, I saw a glimmer of who he really was. His First Boy showed up at the edge of death. I saw vulnerability, love, and pain on his face. It shook me. I saw a boy who'd been abused himself, who'd suffered, and disappeared, who'd become the Hurt Boy and never went back. His pain had been so immense that Hurt Boy ran his life, for the rest of his life. So to see First Boy on his face, in that hospital bed, was a full-circle moment for me.

We all began leaving the hospital room and I was the last to go. As I turned to leave, he said something in a quiet voice, too quiet for me to hear. I came back to his side and leaned over.

"Yes, Dad?" I asked him, coming closer.

"You can take the center of any stage," he told me.

I stayed there momentarily, incredulous at what I'd just heard.

My dad had never spoken into my potential. He'd never asked me what I wanted to do with my life, or what my dreams were. He'd never invested in my future, even refusing to pay for college tuition. I knew he'd loved me, but I'd never heard him speak it.

His final words were the gift I hadn't even realized I needed. I walked away feeling like I'd experienced a transcendent moment, a gift from beyond . . . because I had.

On his last day on earth, he finally spoke the words I'd wanted to hear my whole life. Something in me shifted. A piece of my puzzle clicked back together.

Sitting in the Cave and journaling about this memory, I felt the connection between my past, present, and future getting tighter. First Girl, Hurt Girl, Present Self, Inner Being, and my Future Self sat in that room, and for the first time in my life, I felt whole and complete. My body thrummed with energy, and I sensed that every moment I'd showed up for myself, made a selfish choice, and did the work without knowing the outcome, I was creating the future I'd always been meant to live. I breathed a shaky prayer of gratitude to Dad, the Universe, my family, myself, my children, husband number one, Leo, and every moment of my life, no matter how hard, painful, lonely, confusing, and terrifying, because it had brought me to this very moment, on my couch, in my Cave, feeling free.

Selfish Strategies

There will be times on your Selfish Experiment that you'll find yourself falling back into your old, familiar self. You'll sink back into people-pleasing, or you'll notice those old feelings of guilt and shame coming back. You'll see yourself falling back into old habits and behaviors. Here are some strategies to use when this happens.

Pick Yourself Back Up

There's this thing called homeostasis; it's your body's tendency to go back to its former state. Remember that this is normal. Don't freak out. This is a key part of your growth journey because it's in the falling back that you realize how much you've changed. You can no longer tolerate what used to be normal for you. You're more aware now, and you can't unsee it. When you fall, you never descend to where you were before. At times it may feel like "two steps forward, one step back," but that still means you are making progress. What's more important is that you pick yourself back up, dust yourself off, and begin again. Get back to the rituals and strategies that work for you. Pick up your journal again. Start meditating again. Just get back to the work and don't stress. Remind yourself that this is to be expected and the contraction is preparing you for the next expansion. You've got this!

Release Your Anger

Look. You're a woman living in the patriarchy. Honey, you've got some anger inside. And if you're a woman who was never taught how to feel and process anger in a healthy way, you've got repressed anger. And if you're a woman who was told to be "the good girl," then you *definitely* have repressed anger. So what do you do about it? First, know that holding anger inside is a dangerous game. You are keeping this energy in your body, and after years and decades of stuffing your anger, it starts to eat you alive from the inside out. You will suffer from headaches or migraines; grind your teeth; have jaw pain; have nightmares; avoid conflict; act sarcastic, be passive aggressive, explosive, and uncomfortable with emotions in yourself and others; shut down; tend to complain and obsess; feel bitter, envious, and resentful; and experience guilt and shame. So let's get it out!

- **Big surprise: journaling helps (I know, broken record).** Write out everything you're angry about, who you're angry with, and why. Swear. Rage. Let it out big, then bigger. Write a hate letter to someone. Write about why you're angry at yourself. When you're done, rip it up or burn it. Do not send the letters! This is *your* process, and you need to give yourself permission to be angry.
- **Find a physical outlet.** Start a sport. Kickboxing is fantastic for releasing anger. So is weightlifting. Anger is a powerful energy that gets stored in the body. Release through energetic movement.
- **Meditate (again, broken record).** Meditation builds your ability to remain present, which, over time, will allow you to make more mindful choices when you

Haunted by the Past   155

feel anger rising. Start small. Meditate for five minutes. You can do it!

- **Remove your distraction and coping methods.** There's no better way to get in touch with your anger than to remove the methods you've acquired to repress it. Unplug from all sources of media for 24 hours. Stop eating sugar or drinking alcohol. Stop shopping. Whatever your coping mechanism is, remove it for a time and watch that anger rear its head.
- **Scream into a pillow.** Or go into the woods and throw some rocks. Or go to a rage room – a place specifically designed to release anger, where you get to safely break all sorts of stuff!

Get Out of Survival Mode

Here's what survival mode feels like: depressed, unmotivated, lacking inspiration, stuck in a rut, doing the same things every day, no self-care, no energy, constant worry.

If you're in survival mode, I feel you. It's a terrible place to be, and it can feel impossible to find your way out. It's like you've been dropped into a well, and you're sitting at the bottom, alone, in the dark, the stone walls closing in around you. You can see the light coming in from the top, but it's faint and there's no ladder. So you just sit and wait for it to be over.

Let's handle this, shall we?

- **Make a list.** Write down everything that's draining you. Physical issues? Work problems? Financial situation? Relationship concerns? Make a freaking list.
- **What do you need?** Based on your list, what do you need to prioritize? Maybe it's rest and daily naps.

156 THE SELFISH YEAR

Maybe it's cutting way back on your commitments or socializing. Maybe you need to start budgeting and coming up with a plan to get out of debt. Or hiring someone to help you fine-tune your résumé so you can get out into the work force. Get clear on your next steps.

- **Get support.** Seriously. A majority of my clients come to me when they're in survival mode, and we take care of business. Having support is critical, because you've probably lost perspective. Whether it's a supportive partner, friend, naturopath, therapist, or coach, stop being a lone wolf and ask for the help you need.
- **Start small.** This isn't about overhauling your life in one fell swoop. Your nervous system isn't going to like that. At the same time, doing nothing will get you . . . nothing. You've got to start clawing your way out of the well, and only you can do it. Commit to doing one thing every day that will get you into action. One of my clients committed to walking around her block once every day, and if you knew how deep down the well she was, you'd understand what a herculean task that seemed to her. And she did it. Once around the block, every damn day. After a couple of weeks, she felt a tiny glimmer of . . . something unnamable. Then she started journaling every day. Then she addressed some health issues. She clawed her way out of the fucking well. It took a few months, but she did it. Now she's standing under the clear blue sky, setting goals, dreaming dreams, and taking names.

Client Story

Susan dreamed of opening her own fitness studio in her local city. Her husband didn't support her dream; he had every reason why it wouldn't work, was unrealistic, and was too big a risk. Susan had capitulated to her husband's opinion for years, but couldn't let go of this idea. She had a business plan, she had the expertise, and she had partners who wanted to join her in the venture. And yet she remained stuck in the shadow of her husband's dissent. After a few months, Susan came to a session visibly agitated.

"I'm so fucking pissed off!" she yelled over the Zoom call. "He doesn't want me to succeed. He's threatened by me having something just for myself. I've supported his career for twenty years, and he can't even give me this!"

Susan was getting in touch with years of repressed anger. When her fiery rage died down, she became calm, even serene.

I asked her what she wanted to do.

The answers came fast and clear.

"I'm doing it anyway. I'm going for it. It's my life, it's my money, and he can support me or not. I'll be okay with either. But I'm not holding myself back anymore in fear of what he thinks."

Susan opened the studio six months later. Her husband watched her go for it and saw how he'd been trying to control her because of his fear; he'd been trying to protect her from getting hurt, but it had only served to stifle her magic. Now he's her biggest supporter.

Getting in touch with her anger, releasing it, and expressing it allowed her to get in touch with her Inner Being, and her answers were right there.

Chapter 8

No Risk, No Magic

October brought our third anniversary. Despite our uncertain status, we wanted to celebrate each other and the journey we'd been on both together and separately. We'd met in March of 2013, and since then we had both grown so much. A lot of our growth came from the fact that we triggered each other into our deepest trauma, and therefore had exposed old wounds that neither of us had been aware of before. We were grateful for that, and doing therapy that year had allowed us both to experience deep healing. We wanted to honor that and agreed to meet for dinner.

We met at a little Spanish bistro in a tiny alley in the middle of the city. It seemed fitting to have tapas and wine, an homage to our other home country.

I arrived first and sat at a table on the patio. The autumn evening felt crisp, and the hostess turned on the heater beside me. I fiddled with my napkin, unsure what I wanted to happen that night. The atmosphere was romantic; candles flickered on tables, the cobblestone alley and old stone buildings lent a European feel, and Spanish guitar music played in the background. Did I want romance? My answer came quickly: yes, of course. I was an intensely romantic person. I loved romantic movies, books, and songs and fantasized about having a relationship full of romance and passion. Ours had been that way at first, but after a year or so, we'd both lost our romantic expression for each other. We'd had numerous conversations about this and agreed that while we both wanted romance from each other, neither of us was willing to offer it. The only reason we could come up with was because we wanted to see it from the other person first, which seemed ridiculous, and yet there we sat. Checkmate. Relationships don't always make sense, and this was something that felt absurd and yet completely real. We were stuck in no-man's-land, circling each other, waiting for the other to go first. And neither of us did. It was a sad, unsatisfying game of chicken.

Leo arrived and sat across from me. He looked handsome, and I noticed he'd gotten a haircut. He looked open and happy.

"Happy anniversary," he said.

"Happy anniversary," I replied. We hadn't gotten each other gifts, not because we'd talked about it, but more because it seemed apparent that we weren't in a place to express our hearts to each other.

We ordered dinner and a bottle of wine. Darkness descended on the little alley, and the restaurant filled with other diners. We talked about our favorite subject: our relationship. I noticed that, yet again, we were analyzing and dissecting the last few years. We talked about our childhoods, and Leo shared again his new realizations about where a lot of his dysfunctional communication originated from. I could tell he was deep into the stage of growth where he could now see why he'd been struggling, and yet not at the stage where he could act differently.

I got irritated again; like every other time we focused on what had gone wrong and why. I had very little tolerance left for analysis and found it frustrating, like picking at a scab so it would never heal. I began tearing my paper napkin into tiny pieces and arranging them in a pile on my plate.

"Can we talk about something else?" I said. "This is getting us nowhere."

"Fine," he said, sitting back in his chair.

We sat in silence for a few minutes. Did we really have nothing else to talk about other than our relationship?

"Let's talk about what's good, what's working for us," he said.

No Risk, No Magic

I hesitated. What was working?

"You go first," I said.

He sighed. "Can't you think of anything? You seem obsessed with focusing on the negative."

"That's because our relationship is broken! And until we fix what's not working, we can't enjoy the good parts. We are in major trouble here, and I need to see changes. I'm desperately hoping we can find new ways of being together. We need to create a new foundation. If we can't do that, we don't stand a chance."

He fiddled with his fork. "Well I think there's lots that's working, and if we don't ever talk about the good stuff, we'll just sit in the negative. The only problem here is that you're focusing on what you think isn't working. I want to focus on what is."

"I can't do that right now. I need change." I sighed. "It's like a car with a broken engine. You can't drive it until the engine gets fixed. It might have a beautiful interior, heated seats, brand new brakes, but without an engine . . ." I shrugged. "I need our engine fixed."

He pushed back his chair and left the restaurant without a word.

I sat in stunned silence, staring at the empty chair across from me, the half-eaten meal, the full wine glass. I waited for a few minutes to see if he would come back.

Ten minutes passed. Screw it, I thought. I've been down this road.

Exactly one year before, I'd been in the same situation at a different restaurant in a different city.

He'd surprised me with a weekend trip to Palermo for our first anniversary. It was a place we'd both wanted to see, and he'd gotten a fantastic deal to stay in an old castle. It oozed romance and ambience.

164 THE SELFISH YEAR

The day we were getting ready to go to the airport, we'd gotten into yet another fight that escalated to the point that I locked myself in the bathroom. He stood on the other side, talking to me through the door.

"We need to leave for the airport," he'd said.

"I'm not going. You can go by yourself." I couldn't see any reality where I could go on a romantic weekend.

"Seriously? You're blowing off the trip?"

"I just . . . I can't do it. I can't."

Silence, then I heard the front door open, then close and lock.

He'd gone without me. I felt relief at having space to be alone and massive guilt for bailing on our anniversary trip.

Later that day, I got a text from him.

"I'm here. It's amazing. I wish you were with me. Will you reconsider? There's a later flight today."

I did want to go. I wanted to have a romantic weekend together. Maybe we could forget about the argument and make it work.

I booked the later flight and, filled with hope and trepidation, arrived at our Airbnb in the castle in time for dinner.

We both did our best to let go of the argument and focused on enjoying ourselves, but the tension was thick, at least for me. I found myself walking on eggshells, doing my best to avoid any kind of conversation that would be triggering. But eggshells are fragile ground, and it kept me from being fully present. I wasn't in the place to have sex. I felt irritated and distracted.

And then the inevitable happened. We were having dinner at an incredible restaurant, surrounded by ancient crumbling buildings, untouched after the wartime bombings, making it seem like we were on a movie set. Locals and tourists strolled the streets, enjoying the warm evening, eating gelato and people-watching.

Our conversation ended in a typical argument, and Leo walked out. I sat at the table for a while, then paid our bill and left, wandering through the busy streets back to our rental. I walked in and sat on the bed, watching him in a chair on his phone.

"I think we should spend the rest of the weekend separately," he said, not looking up.

"Okay," I said, a pit forming in my stomach. I didn't have the energy to argue.

And that was it. We spent the next two days on our own, returning to the rental at night and sleeping next to each other without speaking a word. I wandered the streets of Palermo, trying to enjoy myself despite the awareness of how messed up this was. I bought some jewelry at a small boutique and had a delicious lunch at an outdoor café. But I couldn't deny the reality of what we had become – two strangers, sleeping in the same bed, living separate lives. Our self-preservation had become the top priority.

Lesson: If we aren't careful, we can find ourselves tolerating things that we could never imagine. It creeps into our lives like a slow rising tide, and before we know it, we're somewhere we never thought we'd be. Our new normal is so far from where we started, and we're accepting far less than what we deserve – from ourselves and from others.

Sitting at the restaurant in Victoria, eyeing our unfinished meal and feeling the sting of being left behind, I hardened.

I wasn't going to wait to see if he came back. I was done. I paid the bill and walked into the cold night air to see him standing under a streetlight, arms folded against the wind.

"I can't do this anymore," he said.

"Me neither."

"I'm done."

"Me too."

I burst into tears, and he did too. We hugged for a long time.

Finally, I pulled back and wiped my face.

"We both did the best we could," he said.

"I know."

"Can I walk you home?"

"No, that's okay." I turned to go.

"I love you," he said.

"I love you too."

I walked away and didn't look back.

The following day, I lay in bed feeling like shit. I felt like a failure. I felt confused. I felt sad and broken.

I got a text from Leo.

"Hey there. How are you?"

"How am I? We ended our marriage last night."

"I don't see it that way."

"What? How could you not see it that way?"

"I love you. Let's talk about it. We can make this work."

My mind swirled in confusion. What was going on? Why couldn't I decide once and for all? I knew I needed to end this. It had gone on too long as it was. Almost a year separated and months of therapy, and we were still stuck in the same patterns. And yet I couldn't let go. I wasn't ready to make a clean break. Even after last night, I wasn't ready.

No Risk, No Magic 167

If I was going to live by my Selfish Experiment, that meant I had to do what I really wanted. What I really thought was best for me. And what I really wanted was more time. More time to be sure, more time to process, more time to be in this god-awful place of limbo. Being selfish meant I let myself fail, let myself fuck up, let myself do the irrational, because it's what I sensed I needed.

Staying in limbo felt so uncomfortable. I wanted to be anywhere but stuck in this back and forth, and yet I felt like it was what I needed. Part of me – a huge part – wanted to jump back into our marriage and be all in. I knew if I said I was a hundred percent in, that he would be, too. We could rent a place together and pick up where we left off. It was such a tempting idea. My mind wandered to all the great times we'd had together, laughing until we couldn't breathe, making love in the quiet of our room with the Spanish bells ringing outside, planning our next trip, and long talks over bottles of wine about anything and everything. Stay or go? Either way felt impossible still, so the riskiest thing I could choose was to stay in between. And as I was learning, the riskiest choice is usually the perfect one.

I picked up my phone.

"Sure. Let's grab coffee and go to the beach."

I put the phone down and couldn't help but laugh. Despite the pain of last night, I also felt a deep resilience, a deep knowing that this would all work out the way it was meant to, as long as I kept going with my instincts, even when it seemed ridiculous, foolish, or irresponsible. Even if everyone thought I was crazy not to end this. Even if I looked like an idiot, I would finish the year the same way I'd started, walking into the unknown with nothing but my instincts.

168 THE SELFISH YEAR

We agreed to keep working on things. He reassured me that he was all in and was giving a hundred percent to make this work. I believed him. I was, too. And while deep down I sensed that we were nearing the end, I also felt permission to take as long as I needed to be sure. We fell back into our routine of seeing each other a couple of times a week, but this time I requested that we refrain from discussing our relationship. I wanted just to have fun. He agreed, and things felt lighter and easier.

Meanwhile, I felt things shifting within me as I continued connecting to my Inner Being more and more. I wandered down to the beach almost every day, meandering through the parks and streets until I arrived at the coast, then down the long flight of steps that opened onto the pebbled beach. I'd sit on a big driftwood log and stare at the waves coming in and going out relentlessly, without fail. I let my mind wander; sometimes I'd cry, tears mixing with the salt spray from the waves. Other times I'd laugh into the wind.

One day, I noticed a woman walk down to the surf and take off her shoes and socks. She slowly walked into the water until it reached mid-calf, then raised her arms over her head.

The water was frigid, and I wondered what she was up to. Then she began to dance. A wild, whirling, graceful dance, eyes closed, not caring what anyone thought of her. She danced for herself, for the ocean, for the rocks. She danced, and I wished that I was her. She danced for me, too.

I picked up a few rocks, shells, and sea glass for my growing collection and returned home, thanking the Universe for the gift I'd been given that day.

As the year drew to a close, I took inventory, not just of 2020, but of my entire life. I began journaling about it and looking deeply at the choices I'd made. As I did, I noticed something interesting.

I'd gotten married at 19, and we moved to northern British Columbia so he could start a business with money he had borrowed from his parents. Eight months later, we moved back, $200,000 in debt and nothing in our pockets. We moved many more times, as he tried to start a career as a real estate developer. I had my first baby at 25 and had three kids by the time I was 30, with a miscarriage in between. Then I got rheumatic fever, which landed me in the hospital for a week, and required a long recovery that took months. We moved to Phoenix, Kansas City, then back to Canada. I followed my husband without a thought for what I wanted. His career came first, always. The relationship began disintegrating. He cheated on me – multiple times, once with my best friend. His bipolar disorder began getting worse, as well as the drinking. After 24 years, 30 moves, horrible fights, and betrayals, after my codependency and enabling, sweeping things under the rug and hiding the truth, our marriage and family exploded in one terrible day.

We'd hosted a Christmas party for our friends. Great food and of course lots of wine. I watched him drink, and drink, and drink. After everyone left, he continued drinking and I went to bed. Hours later, he collapsed in bed beside me, snoring loudly. He had sleep apnea and wore a mask when he slept, but hadn't put it on. I woke him up and asked him to put the mask on. Before I knew what was happening, he rolled over and started choking me. I screamed, and our son came into the bedroom, pulling him off me. I ran into the bathroom and locked the door, as he tried to break in. Meanwhile, the other kids were hiding in one of the bedrooms.

Eventually, he gave up trying to get to me and went back to bed and passed out. I stayed with the kids, trying to calm them down and reassure them that they were safe.

The next day, I woke up to voices in the kitchen. The kids were talking to him.

"If you want to have a relationship with us, you need to get help," I heard my son saying.

I came into the room just as I heard him say, "Don't worry, you won't have me around to mess up your lives anymore." He walked into the garage.

I knew something was wrong and asked my daughter to drive my youngest son to a friend's home for the day.

I watched them drive away, and as I walked back in the house, Jordan came to meet me, his face pale.

"Dad tried to hang himself in the garage."

"What?"

"He was on a ladder with an electrical cord. I talked him down."

I grabbed my phone and dialed 911. Soon our driveway was full of police cars, fire trucks, and an ambulance. We were *that* house.

The police took him to the psychiatric ward, and before they left, one of them pulled me aside. He looked straight in my eyes and said, "I don't want to come back here one day and have to deal with a different outcome."

I nodded. I knew exactly what he meant.

I called his family and told them to come and get him. He never came home. I'd waited until the last possible moment to end the marriage, always hoping and waiting for change, which never came. This nail in the coffin came at a huge price for my children. I'd waited too long and would have to live with that. Seeing the traumatic looks on their faces destroyed me, knowing that my lack of boundaries had contributed to that.

No Risk, No Magic 171

And now, here I sat in the Cave, staring at an account of my adult life, and realizing I'd never considered what I'd chosen, what happened, and the cost of it all.

I wrote:

> "Wow. I guess I'd never seen my life as overly stressful. When I look at it on the page, I've always been in a state of stress. "Highly resilient," a therapist once told me. One of the most resilient people he'd ever met. I took that as a badge of honor; my ability to withstand chaos and trauma. I'd learned it when I was eight. It's my way of life."

Something shifted inside me; I felt pieces of me falling off, like the dream I'd had with the white scales that would only fall away when they were ready. I felt a shedding of my old self like never before; the old, resilient me was dying.

Fuck resilience. I don't want it anymore. I don't want to be "the strong one," "the glue" that holds everyone else together. I want to be soft and tender. I want to feel my heart break from the beauty and ugliness of the world. I want to long for things. I want to ache and break. I want to soar with ecstasy and wail with despair. I'm done being numb, distracted, shut down, and dead inside. I'm done with the coping mechanisms: the drink, the food, the moving, the relationships. I'm done ignoring my true self for the sake of the status quo, not rocking the boat, staying safe, and keeping others happy. I'm done with all of it. I want to howl at the moon, dance naked under the stars, light up the world, throw my hands to the sky, walk into the cold ocean and let it cleanse me of my past. I want to be free, I want to feel, and I want, more than anything, to finally feel at home inside of myself.

The next morning I headed out for my walk as usual, turned toward the park and said to myself, "I deserve to be happy."

172   THE SELFISH YEAR

I stopped on the sidewalk, stunned. Sure, I'd said this before. I'd been saying it to myself for years. And yet I'd only ever found fleeting moments of happiness in between all the shitty feelings. I'd said it, but never fully believed it.

And yet on this ordinary November morning, I said it without hesitation, with conviction, with absolute knowing.

"I deserve to be happy, goddammit!"

I resumed walking but with a new spring in my step. I put my headphones on and played "Bird Set Free."

"I fucking deserve to be happy!"

I played the song on repeat and let myself cry and sob and pant as I marched to the beat of a new day.

"I deserve life to be easy. It gets to be easy, because I'm worthy, and I'm worthy because I'm alive!"

The lightness, the freedom, the joy, flowed into me and through me and it felt like the whole world rejoiced with me. The trees danced just for me. The people smiled at me. The waves sang their song for me. My emancipation carried me to new heights and I was ready.

I'd never considered magic before. Living a magical life hadn't been a goal, a priority, or even a consideration. As a card-carrying member of the People-Pleasers Club, I'd prided myself on my pragmatism and realistic outlook on life. I was the voice of reason, the stable friend, the one people would come to for advice and a reality check. I didn't entertain dreaming or magic; it didn't fit into my reality. My reality was responsibility, duty, getting shit done, and cleaning up other people's messes.

The only time I opened to magic was with my children. When they were little, we had so much magic together. I loved being a full-time mom, and almost every day there would be an opportunity to create magic for them. Giving them magic was easy. I'd put on some music, and we

No Risk, No Magic

would dance and march around the house, falling into piles of laughter. We'd jump on the trampoline in the rain, build forts in the living room, and play dress-up and make-believe. I'd pack a lunch and we'd go to the beach, picking shells and making driftwood castles. We'd spend hours at the park or in the forest telling stories to each other. Witnessing their first steps, pulling them close when they fell, reading stories to them every night, singing songs and rubbing backs, washing hair and drying tears; being a mother was magical. My kids were magical.

Creating magic *within me* was different. I didn't know how to do it; I hadn't even considered it as an option. I lived in reality and did a great job at getting things done. Magic and dreaming were for flaky people, irresponsible people, indulgent people. Not me.

I had tricked myself into thinking that I had created a magical life. Everything I'd chosen in the last few years had seemed magical at the time. It had seemed adventurous and glamorous and exciting. And while some of it was, for sure, it wasn't magical. I might have been living a life of external pleasures and adventure, but inside there was no magic, only tumbleweeds blowing around. I'd believed that magic was found outside of myself, in things, in people, in experiences.

What I realized now was that magic is found within, and it can only be created by me. Nobody and nothing can make my life magical. And the way I'd created magic for myself was a strange alchemy that I could have never discovered through rational and logical thought. Because magic only happened when I stayed with myself, listened to and trusted myself. Magic happened when I took the risk to show up for myself and act on my intuition. It happened when I obeyed the call of my Inner Being and took action

174 THE SELFISH YEAR

on what I heard. It happened when I stopped abandoning First Girl and when I started healing Hurt Girl. It happened when I felt my whole feelings and got really honest with myself. It happened when I did the scary things I'd been running from my entire life. It happened when I stopped running and sat still.

Then the magic came, but it came slowly, like fireflies winking as the dusk falls. Every time I took a risk to stay with myself, another firefly would light up. Tiny dots of light inside that illuminated the darkness. Day by day, over the year, more light showed up. Glimmers of hope. Moments of belief. Seconds of joy. Minutes of happiness. More self-trust, self-belief, faith, self-love, pride, creativity, inspiration. Ideas would come to me in the early morning hours. I started dancing in my Cave to music that made me feel alive. I filled my journal with pages of declarations about my future.

I started looking up at the trees when I walked instead of down at the ground. I'd look up, and the tall Douglas firs would look down at me, and I felt a connection. Placing my hands on my heart, I would talk to them, whispering my secrets. I'd touch their gnarled, mossy trunks and feel their energy mixing with mine. I began skipping when I walked or raising my hands to the sky as I listened to music. I found myself wanting to eat healthier foods and drink less wine. I needed less sleep and would often awake in the early morning hours, buzzing with ideas that I would write in my journal by candlelight. Gratitude came easier, and instead of just writing out the same three things in my gratitude journal every day, I started filling pages; it poured out of me.

Living a magical life isn't a flaky, unrealistic pipe dream. It's the way we are meant to live. It's how we're meant to

No Risk, No Magic 175

feel, all the time. I found magic in my past, as I looked at my life and everything that had happened to me, and that I'd chosen. Everything I'd been through, good and bad, joyful and painful, had brought me to this moment. I saw the magic in all of it. Because magic isn't just about the good times, or the good feelings. It's also about the devastating, painful, challenging, and brutal times that feel like darkness and desert when we are in it. But we're given a choice. We can stay in the desert, existing in the empty nothingness, or we can take the risk to face it with courage. Even though we may be shaking inside, we walk into the alchemy of healing, of being honest with ourselves and others, of facing the dark parts of ourselves that we don't want to look at, and allowing it to transform us. The risk that is required is to stop running from ourselves and face the shadow. Face Hurt Girl and offer her what she's always needed: safety. The risk is to sit with ourselves long enough to hear the truth and then do it again, and again, and again, until the fireflies start to appear. Magic lives inside of us, all the time. We've just stopped looking.

No risk, no magic.

My whole year had been about risking, yet here I was, near the end of my experiment, still risking, still scared, still choosing myself. It's not that it became less risky; in fact, it felt like the risks were getting increasingly bigger. The difference was that I trusted the process more. I believed that risk got me what I wanted. And the riskiest choice of all would be to stay in the fire of indecision and in between until I felt my Inner Being tell me differently. Sometimes, risk isn't about making big moves; sometimes, the biggest risk is to stay in the fire and let yourself burn without running, escaping, numbing, or distracting. Sit in the fire of your indecision, your not knowing, the uncertainty, and

176 THE SELFISH YEAR

allow the fire to burn away everything that wants to run for the hills. And trust that you will burn for as long as you need to, until the ashes of your old self pile at your feet, and you walk into your future clear eyed, determined, and soaring on wings that carry you to uncharted lands.

Selfish Strategies

Let's talk about two F-words: Failure and Fulfillment. You might be surprised to know that you can't have one without the other. Let's go!

Let Yourself Fail

Does the idea of failing freak you out? It does most people! We've been conditioned to believe that failure is bad, shameful, the worst thing that could happen. We learn to protect ourselves from failing so we never have to feel these bad feelings. We become measured, controlled; we anticipate possible outcomes and adjust accordingly. Can you relate? Have you censored, edited, and curated your life to protect yourself from failure? Does the very idea of failing give you the sweats?

Your nervous system doesn't like discomfort or fear. Whenever you consider stepping into something uncomfortable, your nervous system gets activated, and then your brain perceives that you are in danger and kicks into survival mode. Now you're in fight, flight, freeze or fawn. You are focused on keeping yourself safe. This is what happens when you want to create big changes or go for scary things in life, and this part of your brain, in all its misguided concern for your safety, is sabotaging you. It's keeping you small so you will never fail.

No Risk, No Magic

And yet failure is a part of the equation of success. You cannot succeed without failure. Look at toddlers learning to walk. They walk a few steps and fall. Get back up, walk a few steps, and fall – over and over until they can walk, then run.

It's time to change your relationship with failure. Once you see that failure is essential to your success, to your growth, to you getting the life you want and feeling the way you want, you will begin to open to the idea that failure doesn't mean what you have always believed.

Your subconscious will begin to shift its belief about failure. You'll see that failure is only feedback; it's valuable information for the next time you step into discomfort and fear. Failure is your friend, your ally. It builds resilience, grit, and determination. It challenges your beliefs about where your value lies. Failure offers you the gift of growth.

I dare you to Google some of your heroes, and find out how many times they failed on their journey to success. Get real about what it required. Start to change your thinking about what failure means. Let go of the emotional charge around it. Open to the idea that failure is likely the best thing to ever happen to you.

Once you believe this, you're unstoppable. You won't let anything stand in your way. You'll take bigger risks, you'll make bold moves, and you'll do things that surprise the hell out of you. You'll look in the mirror and say, "Who is this powerhouse of a woman!?"

So how do you get there? Micro changes, baby!

Small steps into risk and a willingness to fail in small ways will build your resilience and grit.

THE SELFISH YEAR

This is where the rubber meets the road. It's time to make some moves. Journal time!

- If you knew you couldn't fail, what would you do? Come on, get real, get big, get crazy! Let your First Girl loose on the pages because she's the one with all the big dreams. Write it all down with wild abandon.
- Build your belief that failure is necessary for success. Write about your heroes and how they failed. Start gathering evidence that failure is your friend and ally.
- Write out all your fears about failing. There's no point in avoiding the fears; that guarantees they'll stick around. Write it all down.
- Now write about what you decide that you get to have in your life. Maybe you decide that you get to be happy or you get to be wealthy. You can decide that you get to travel the world, start a business, or fall in love. Decide that you get to be selfish. Decide that you get to have a beautiful garden, or a great relationship with your kids. Whatever. Just write it out and declare it. It doesn't matter if you "feel" it or not. Don't wait to believe it before you do it; it doesn't work like that. Decide and declare first every damn day, and the belief will follow. I promise. This is faith: believing in something that doesn't exist yet.
- What is *one* action step you will take this week that feels like leaning into failure? A small step into fear? Write it down. Then do it. And the next week, do one more step. And then next. If you take one tiny step into discomfort each week, at the end of a year, you will have taken 52 steps toward your dreams. And you will be farther down the path than you are today. And if you fail? Amazing! Celebrate!

Fulfillment Is a Radical Act

It really is. It takes intention and determination to create a fulfilling and happy life. The world is not handing it to you or to anyone else. A lot of the world around you is conspiring to make you unhappy. Every advertisement is banking on your unhappiness so they can sell you something you think will make you happy. They are reminding you that you're dissatisfied. Social media is saturating you with images that make you feel less than worthy, less beautiful, that you need to look like someone else, that who you are or the life you have isn't okay. News stations are inundating you with fear and misery. Addiction to news is one of the most pervasive contributors to anxiety and depression.

The patriarchy has kept women oppressed and suppressed. We are swimming upstream if we want to feel fulfilled. So if you're reading this book, you are a rare breed. You're willing to regain your power and build a life that turns you on. And it will not only change your life, but the ripple effect will travel through generations. You are doing this for you first, but also for the generations after you.

A Magical Life Is Your Birthright

You deserve to wake up each morning filled with wonder and delight, excited at the day ahead. But if you want it, you will have to work for it. It won't drop in your lap, and it won't come to you from a weekend retreat or from reading this book. I am giving you the tools to create it, but you have to do the work for yourself.

180 THE SELFISH YEAR

This happens incrementally; that's why micro changes are so powerful. It happens in the thousand tiny decisions you make each day. It happens when you take your power back over your morning, and instead of going on your phone right away, you start meditating, journaling, or practicing yoga. It happens when you turn off the news and play music that gets you dancing. It happens when you work with a guide who challenges and holds you accountable. It happens when you have hard conversations with love and grace, when you set boundaries for yourself, when you say no. It happens when you say what you want, when you teach others how to treat you, and when you stop settling for crumbs from someone else and make a feast for yourself.

Magic happens when you take risks, do scary things, and build your courage. Magic happens when you heal your Hurt Girl so she feels safe enough to let you dream again. It happens when you let First Girl have a voice again, to talk to you about what she wants and how she wants to play and be free. It happens every time you look in the mirror and say something kind. It happens in all of these tiny moments, one after another, like pearls on a necklace. You are building a magical life in each moment.

And then one day you'll be walking down the street, and you'll feel happy, free, and excited, and you'll realize: *You're doing it*. You're building a life that you're proud of, that excites you, and it's unfolding right in front of you.

- There is no better feeling than this.
- Show up for yourself every day.
- Keep doing these small steps every day.
- Keep being selfish every day.
- This is how you become fulfilled, magical, free, and happy.

Client Story

Jessica had tried to leave her husband eight times, and each time she went back. She reached out to me because she knew she wouldn't do it on her own. She needed support.

After 30 years of marriage and raising two kids together, their relationship had slowly deteriorated and they now lived more like roommates. She described their communication like this:

"He doesn't leave me alone. If I'm working in the office, he barges in and yells at me. I have no privacy, no space. I can't take it anymore. He guilts me into staying, tells me I'm all he has. I don't think I even like him anymore. I feel like a terrible person for wanting to leave, but I've become a ghost in this marriage."

Jessica and I spent some time getting clear on the status of the relationship, so that she could see exactly what was happening. I told her to look at everything as data: information that would help her to make a wise decision. She learned about emotional abuse and agreed that this is what she'd been experiencing for years. We examined everything she'd tried to do up to this point to save the marriage. Her husband had refused to go to therapy, so she went alone. She'd asked for the changes she needed: healthy communication, respect, kindness. It wasn't happening.

Jessica knew the marriage was over; she'd known it each time she'd tried to leave previously. Now she had the information she needed to feel even more certain that the best choice for her was to leave.

We discussed her exit strategy. She was afraid to tell him that she wanted a divorce. He was known to go into rages

(continued)

182 THE SELFISH YEAR

(continued)

when he didn't get his way. She didn't think he'd get violent, but she was terrified to tell him.

Meanwhile, she had rented a storage unit nearby, and every day when he was at work, she took some of her belongings there. Little by little she gathered what she needed and prepared to leave. She rented an Airbnb in another state for a month, so she could have a safe place to land and determine her next moves.

We decided on the day she was going to leave. She didn't know how to tell him; if she had a face-to-face conversation, she was worried that he would physically keep her from leaving. And yet she felt terrible leaving a note. That felt like a cowardly thing to do and she knew it would hurt him.

I reminded Jessica that her safety was the most important thing. Once she was out, they could talk and she could say everything she needed to say. She agreed and wrote a note that she planned to leave on the morning she moved out.

That morning, Jessica called me. I could barely understand her, she was so upset.

"I can't leave. I can't do this to him. I feel terrible," she said through sobs.

"Jessica," I said, "you know this is the right thing to do. Everything in you is screaming at you to stay right where you are, because it's all you've known for over thirty years. But you know that if you stay, you'll never get the chance to have the life you deserve. To be happy, and free, and at peace. All the things you've told me you desperately want."

"I know," she said. "But I'm so scared. I'm terrified to walk out that door."

I reminded her of something I'd told her before, about doing scary things: It can feel scary to imagine doing something hard. But imagining it isn't the scary part. It's the anticipation of doing the scary thing. Often, all you really need is ten seconds of insane courage.

She promised me that she would do it and hung up.

A little while later, I got a message from Jessica. It was a picture of her, in her car, the dogs in the back seat, on the side of the road.

She did it.

Her face was blotchy and swollen from tears, and she wasn't smiling, but I could see it in her eyes.

She'd set herself free.

Chapter 9

Bird Set Free

Christmas approached and brought the gift of more emotional baggage to unwrap.

The traumatizing ending to my marriage with husband number one, which resulted in his suicide attempt, had happened just a few days before Christmas. That year, the kids and I tried to celebrate as usual; we opened gifts and had a turkey dinner, all of us putting on brave smiles, but none of us could ignore the wreckage of our family that lay among the piles of crumpled wrapping paper. We'd planned a ski trip between Christmas and New Year's; we still went and I spent most of the time lying on my bed in the dark while the kids went skiing and tubing.

Now it was the end of my Selfish Year, and I found myself dreading Christmas. Most of Canada was still shut down due to the ongoing pandemic, and travel was discouraged. The kids and I had agreed to stay in our respective cities over the holidays. I knew this was the right choice, and I also dreaded being alone. At the same time, I'd never spent a Christmas by myself and knew that the Universe would most likely have some lessons for me to learn.

By this time I was used to seeing everything as a growth opportunity. When things didn't go the way I'd hoped, instead of getting upset and trying to force a different outcome, I practiced acceptance and seeing the meaning in it. I'd discovered that meaning is everything. What happened or didn't happen was neutral; the meaning I attached to it made all the difference in my experience. I could look back on the year and see that every time I accepted what happened and didn't place a meaning on it, I felt much happier, freer, and more open to solutions. My old negative-focused, worrying, and anxious self began disappearing each time I practiced nonattachment.

188   THE SELFISH YEAR

Leo and I talked about Christmas and whether we would spend it together. I wanted to spend Christmas Day together because that would be the most challenging day for me to be alone. We decided that he would come to my place for brunch, and then we would walk to his place and cook dinner there.

"Do you want to buy gifts for each other?" I asked him one day as we walked to the beach. Nothing made sense in our relationship anymore; after being separated for almost a year, there was no room for assumptions.

"No, let's not," he said. "If we're not together, what's the point?"

"Okay," I replied.

One evening a few days later, he called me.

"I changed my mind. Let's buy gifts for each other. I love you, and I want to celebrate that."

Surprised but pleased, I agreed.

What do you give your husband who lives in the same city but in a different home, from whom you've been separated for a year, but you're in therapy, and you see the end of the relationship looming, but you're not ready to pull the trigger? Does Hallmark make a card for that?

I bought him a couple of very nice shirts that I knew would look good on him. Thoughtful but unsentimental. Perfect.

Christmas Day arrived, and I FaceTimed with the kids while we opened our gifts to each other. I didn't tell them that I'd spent the morning crying. I missed them, and my heart ached. I missed having a home, a real home that my kids could come and hang out at. I still struggled with the feeling that I'd abandoned them by moving away. Everything in me screamed that I was a bad mother, that this whole year had been a joke, a mistake. That I was a fraud and

Bird Set Free

being selfish was bullshit. The guilt over choosing myself that year loomed large, and I curled into a ball on my bed and cried.

I could never have anticipated how hard it would be to choose myself. Well aware that my situation allowed me to live alone, travel, and have extravagant amounts of time to myself, I began to question the validity of this experiment. Could I have done this 10 or 20 years ago, when I had small kids, no job, and a toxic relationship? Leaving Spain and living alone in Victoria gave me the ability to dig deep into myself and gave me the space to do deep inner work. Was this just a deluded act of privilege? Who was I kidding?

I sunk lower into the abyss of guilt and shame and began to question everything. What the hell was I doing, leaving my marriage like this? I looked around at the Cave, dark and quiet in the early morning. Why am I here? I left a perfectly good apartment in Valencia and a fantastic life. I drank wine on a Tuesday afternoon at outdoor cafés. I bicycled to the beach and ate paella next to the Mediterranean. I roamed the cobblestone alleys in the summer heat, listening to flamenco music drift from a nearby square. I made love in my gorgeous bed with the shutters thrown open to the cool night air and fell asleep in the arms of a good man.

Everything I'd walked away from piled on top of me that morning, and I felt like I would suffocate from the weight of my actions. I'd hurt Leo, hurt him deeply. I had been getting questions and comments from his family and mine, wondering what was happening. I was pretty sure they thought I'd had a breakdown or a midlife crisis. Maybe they were right. Perhaps that's all this was: a typical middle-aged woman throwing her life away because she was bored, blowing up her marriage and world because she wanted something different.

I thought about the hours and days and weeks I'd spent over the past year journaling, meditating, walking, sitting at the beach, and now it seemed foolish and indulgent. The hot flush of shame rose up my chest, and I clutched my stomach.

Maybe it was all a lie. Perhaps choosing selfish as my word for the year was a delusion brought on by my misery. Perhaps I'd been fooling myself into thinking that I deserved anything different from what I'd had, and maybe I wasn't being led by my Inner Being but my basic desire to feel special. Why did I think I deserved anything more? Who was I to want more? Was I taking everything for granted? Looking for problems where they don't exist?

I began thinking about all the good times, laughing until we couldn't breathe, making love in the quiet nights, the way he wrapped me in his arms, our inside jokes. Was I prepared to throw it all away? The idea of being alone terrified me. My solitude over the last year had been tolerable because I still had a marriage I could jump back into at any time. I wasn't really alone. We were still married, still working on our relationship. I had options.

I could go back. I could go all in, give all of myself to him again, and really work on it. Maybe if I committed wholeheartedly, forgot all the shit we'd gone through, and focused on the positive like he kept telling me, we could make it work. Perhaps the problem was me, and now that I'd spent time working on myself, things would be better. Maybe now that I'd done so much healing, now that I'd found happiness within myself, and I had let go of looking for it outside, I could be truly happy with him, too.

I showered, pulled on a pair of jeans and a sweater, and started getting brunch ready. As I chopped strawberries for the French toast, I pictured us back together, living a happy married life. Perhaps that was the whole point of this year; I'd finally found happiness inside of myself, so now we could find happiness together. It made sense. It lined up with all the conversations we'd had over the past couple of years.

I remembered one sweltering afternoon when we'd sat together on our patio in Valencia. We'd talked for hours, as usual, and I'd had to fight to keep my emotions in check.

"You're not happy," he'd said to me.

"I am, I'm a happy person," I replied. "I'm just struggling with us. The conflict is wearing me down."

"It's not about the conflict. It's because you aren't happy. You're one of the most miserable people I've ever met."

My mouth dropped open.

"I can't believe you just said that."

"It's true," he said, taking a long drink of his beer. I watched the condensation dripping off the glass, leaving a puddle on the table.

"You're an angry person. You're not happy. So of course you can't find anything good about our relationship."

I threw the strawberries into the bowl and got the eggs from the fridge. Maybe he was right. I was prepared to take all the responsibility for our problems. I wanted this marriage to work. I pictured our life together, both of us happy and content, and it felt like a dream. I wanted that dream.

I looked around the Cave: no Christmas tree or lights, barely any furniture. I could walk from the front door to the back patio in 20 steps. My dishes, cutlery, and pots were from the Dollar Store. Instead of seeing the comfort and safety I'd experienced all year, I saw a pathetic little hole I'd been hiding in. It reeked of sadness and isolation, confusion and denial.

Our therapist had said something to me in one of our private sessions that stood out.

"Everything is data, Val," she'd said. "Everything that happens is giving you information. Take the data and use it to show you what's really going on."

Lesson: Perspective is reality. What you experience is a result of the stories you're telling yourself about what's happening. And while what's happening might be painful, devastating, or terrifying, that's not the only story that's available. It might also be a heroic tale of your triumph. You can rewrite the story anytime you want. Be the villain, or the rock star, or the crazy lady singing to herself. It's your story. Write one that inspires you.

I decided to try it that day. I needed to feel what it would be like to be back together again. I needed to feel hopeful that we could make it, that we'd both grown enough to create a solid foundation going forward. We couldn't go back to the way we were; we both agreed about that. To go forward, we had to create something new, something real, something safe. I needed a sign that this was possible. If I got some data that showed me we were getting there, then I would do it. I'd go all in and we would try again.

I dipped bread into the eggy mixture and whispered a prayer to the Universe:

"Show me a sign. I need one. I need one now."

Leo arrived, and we hugged. I felt the warmth of his arms around me and softened into the embrace.

As I turned to serve the food onto plates, he sat on the couch.

"I didn't get you a gift," he said.

"Oh?" I replied, keeping my voice neutral despite the instant twist in my gut.

"I didn't have time. I've been busy looking for work."

This didn't surprise me, and yet I felt a hot flush of anger in my chest.

"Well, I got you a gift. That was our agreement, right?" I grabbed his gifts from the bed and handed them to him.

"I'm sorry," he said.

"I'm disappointed," I replied. "It was your idea to buy gifts for each other."

"I know." Tears filled his eyes.

"Well, go ahead and open yours."

He tore the wrapping paper and pulled out the shirts.

"Wow, so awesome. I love them, babe. Thank you."

"You're welcome," I said.

"Like I said, I just didn't have time."

I sighed. "I don't believe you."

"Why?"

"Because it's bullshit. We agreed on this last week. You're telling me you didn't have time to go to a store in the last week? You couldn't have stopped at a gas station or the drugstore? Bought me a cheap candle or some flowers? A bottle of wine?"

He looked surprised.

"I'm sorry. I had good intentions."

"I don't want to hear about your intentions. I want you to know how your actions impacted me."

"I'm sorry you feel upset."

"Just stop." I held up a hand. "Let's not do this. I want to just enjoy the day."

We carried on in silence and later walked to his apartment, cooked a simple meal, and watched a movie.

194   THE SELFISH YEAR

The movie ended and darkness had fallen. I considered my options: walk home in the cold, or spend the night. Surprisingly, staying felt like the most uncomfortable choice.

"How would you feel if I spent the night?" I couldn't believe how much effort it took to ask the question. However, I figured that if I really wanted a sign, if I really wanted to know for sure if we could move forward, this might help things along.

"Sure," he said and began to tidy the kitchen.

I sat on the couch feeling like a teenager on a first date.

He found a T-shirt for me to wear, and we climbed into his bed, each taking the respective sides that we'd always slept on. It felt utterly familiar and, at the same time, devastatingly foreign.

I lay on my back, staring at the ceiling in the dark, quiet night. He did the same. We hadn't spoken since we got into bed, and my mind went crazy.

What is he thinking? Why is he so quiet? I'd hoped for some kind of conversation about what this meant or what we wanted out of this, but the words wouldn't come. I didn't want sex, but a cuddle would have felt nice after so many months apart.

His breathing evened out, and I knew he was asleep. I looked over at his silhouette in the dark of the bedroom. I'd memorized every feature: the small lines at the corners of his eyes, the sharp profile of his nose, the strong chin.

I rolled on my side, trying to will myself to sleep by counting backward from 100. It was a trick I'd learned years ago to override my bedtime anxiety, but this time no amount of counting worked to silence my thoughts or calm my racing heart.

The longer I lay there, the worse I felt. Nothing in me wanted to get up and walk home in the middle of the night, so I tried to stick it out.

I'd become so good at shutting off my feelings. My eight-year-old self learned how to turn it off and compartmentalize pain. Ever since, I'd had a solid ability to continue in situations that were dangerous, unpleasant, or simply not what I wanted. I could endure horrible conflict, traumatic events, and deep pain because I knew how to cut it off from myself. Abandoning myself had worked for me when I couldn't face reality. It had also kept me in situations far longer than I should have stayed.

I didn't want to be resilient anymore. I wanted to be soft, open, and tender. I wanted to feel deeply and know when to take my leave. I wanted to take care of myself first, to trust that my experience mattered and that I would tend to the little girl inside who only ever wanted to feel safe.

At that moment, I knew what I needed to do. I did trust myself, more than ever before. I listened to my First Girl asking for safety, not from Leo but from Hurt Girl, who had been making all the decisions for us. Hurt Girl told me to stay, to override my needs, to abandon myself and not disrupt the situation. Hurt Girl told me to stay quiet and power through. Hurt Girl was the resilient one, and she'd had to be to survive. She'd done a great job protecting us by keeping the shield up, yielding the sword, and guarding the gate.

The difference, on that quiet Christmas night, was not the situation. The difference was me. I realized at that moment, lying next to my husband, that everything I'd gone through that year wasn't about him, or us, or our relationship. I hadn't walked away from *him*. I'd walked away from my old self, from my patterns, coping mechanisms, and denial. I'd walked away from the choices that Hurt Girl had made because her choices created hurt for me and everyone else. Her fearful self-protection was not only no longer needed, but it was also no longer sustainable.

I listened to my body that night, telling me it needed my help to feel safe. I listened to Hurt Girl, telling me to suppress my feelings and override my intuition. I listened to First Girl telling me she needed to leave. I watched it all like I was outside my body, floating to the ceiling, observing the battle. I watched it all happening inside, without judging myself or losing myself in it.

I heard another voice, quiet and still and serene, join the fray.

This is the sign you asked for. Pay attention.

Immediately, all the other voices subsided, and everything got calm. I tuned into this voice that felt like a ringing bell inside my being: clear, bright and true.

I know. I know. I know.

Sliding off the bed, I took off his shirt and put on my own clothes. He stirred next to me.

"I'm going to go home," I whispered in the quiet room.

"Okay," he replied.

I grabbed my purse and phone and silently left his apartment, squinting in the bright light of the hallway as I punched the elevator button and rode down to the lobby. Walking through the front doors and into the street, I checked my phone for the time: 11:50 p.m.

I walked the dark streets home at the end of Christmas Day, feeling a thousand emotions:

- **Pride.** I'd shown up for myself like never before.
- **Certainty.** For the first time in a year I knew what I needed from a relationship.
- **Fear.** Walking into an unknown future.
- **Trust.** Beyond a shadow of a doubt, I trusted myself.
- **Excitement.** For the first time in a very long time, I felt goosebumps when I imagined what lay ahead.

- **Sadness.** Walking away meant leaving behind a good person. And it meant letting go of the future we'd dreamed of together.
- **Confidence.** I'd given a hundred percent to the process.
- **Freedom.** I'd emancipated myself from living life for everyone else.

Looking up at the night sky, I drew a shaky, deep breath, and as I gazed at the starry blanket above me, I sang out loud the words that had walked me from Spain to Paris, to Canada, and now, home to myself.

And I don't care if I sing off-key
I find myself in my melodies
I sing for love, I sing for me
I shout it out like a bird set free
I'll shout it out like a bird set free

I walked into the Cave and, in the dark silence of my tiny home, I dropped to my knees and wept, tears falling to the floor. I looked around and saw it so clearly; it wasn't a depressing, dark hole of self-indulgence. It was a sanctuary, a soft, safe place for me to land. I wept tears of gratitude as I looked around at what I'd created, by me, for me. It didn't matter that my furniture was haphazardly built with one tiny screwdriver. I didn't care that I only had two plates and two bowls or that my end table was a cardboard box. I didn't miss my glamorous Spanish apartment because my freedom meant more. I'd rather be free in this little home that I built than captive to misery in a mansion.

I put my head in my hands on the floor and whispered to myself, "Thank you. Thank you. Thank you."

For the first time in my life, I was home.

Selfish Strategies

I'm guessing you've been looking for a reason.

A reason to leave your relationship, or to set a boundary, or to speak the truth.

A reason to say "no," or to end a friendship.

A reason to be selfish, put yourself first, prioritize your needs.

A reason to do what you enjoy, to rest, to stop making everyone else happy when you're miserable.

A reason to do what really matters to you.

A reason to disappoint other people so you don't disappoint yourself.

A reason to drop the mask, to stop fixing, rescuing, and enabling, to let things fall apart, and to finally be free.

You're looking for a reason to justify being selfish, and maybe you can't find one. If only he was "a bad guy," or if only she was "a bitch," or if only the kids were grown up, or you had more money, more time, more confidence.

Here's what I want you to know:

You are the reason.

That's it.

Your happiness is the only reason you need.

I know it's hard, because you've been told that you need to justify making choices just because they're right for you.

But I also know that you've been doing the work to unravel all the old patterns and lies.

I know that you are coming home to yourself.

I know that you are unlearning who you aren't, and learning who you are.

I know that your First Girl needs you to keep her safe, and your Hurt Girl is tired of doing all the work.

I know you are ready to be selfish. It's time to start your own Selfish Experiment.

And as you do, you'll see how powerful you are. Powerful to create a safe home inside yourself, where you have everything you need. Powerful to make choices that are right for you. Powerful to trust yourself. Powerful to change your thoughts, to process your emotions, to take new action.

You are powerful, and as you learn how to be selfish, everything will fall into place.

You will give to your people from overflow and abundance.

It will become a joy to love others.

You'll be happier than you can even imagine.

Your relationships will transform because you have transformed.

You are the reason.

Do it for you.

Client Story

"How the hell am I supposed to be 'selfish' when I'm raising three little kids, my husband works out of town every two weeks, and I barely have time to shower, let alone do all this work on myself?"

Lexi glared at me through the computer screen; I could feel the heat of her rage.

She'd gotten married at 22, was pregnant at 25, and by 30 she had three kids under three. Now, at 35, Lexi was drowning in diapers, preschool drop-offs, laundry, and constant demands on her time and attention.

And yet here she sat across from me.

"Why are you here?" I asked her.

(continued)

(continued)

Tears sprang from her eyes.

*"I'm here because I'm fucking angry that this is my life."
She swiped at her cheeks. "Like, I get it . . . I chose it. I made
the decision to have kids. And I love being a mom, I do.
But . . . I hate it too. I miss the old me, the fun me. I miss
having time to enjoy a glass of wine in the evenings by myself.
I miss sleeping through the night."*

*Lexi was caught in a trap of her own making, and now
she had no idea what to do.*

*"Lexi, this isn't about time, or the lack of it. It's not
about you being too busy to be selfish. And it's not about
your kids."*

"Okay . . ." she said. "So what is it about?"

"That's what we're going to find out, together."

*For the next few months, Lexi and I got curious about
why she felt so angry. She began to realize that the person she
was angry with was herself. She was furious that she'd agreed
to get married so young, instead of going to college. She was
angry that she'd had kids so quickly instead of spending her
20s having fun and traveling. And she was angry with herself
for being angry. The guilt she felt was huge. Mothers aren't
supposed to feel this way.*

But they do, and she did.

*First order of business? Forgiving herself. We worked
through the process of forgiving the younger version of herself
for making the choices that she did. She began to see that
she'd done the best she could at the time, with what she knew.
And she began to feel compassion for that younger Lexi.*

*Next? Be willing to ask for support. She'd been working
so hard at taking care of everything herself, being strong, that*

she failed to see that she had help waiting in the wings: aka her mother-in-law. Instead of taking her up on the numerous offers to help out with childcare and cooking meals, she'd always declined, not wanting to admit that she couldn't handle it. Lexi reached out to her mother-in-law and asked for help.

These two steps created major shifts for Lexi. Her rage subsided and she began to feel calmer, more grounded. Life was still busy, for sure. But she was learning how to take care of herself in the most basic of ways, that made massive differences.

Being selfish doesn't have to take a lot of time. Sometimes all it takes is one different choice that changes so much.

Epilogue

I'm writing this from bed – yes, the bed I built all by myself. But now it's sitting in a beautiful apartment on the 27th floor overlooking downtown Vancouver. The sun is streaming through the big windows, illuminating the plants, paintings, and stacks of books in the corner. Sia is playing on the Bluetooth speaker, but now the song that's on repeat is not "Bird Set Free," but "Unstoppable."

I go to the kitchen, pour another cup of coffee from the French press, and sink into my overstuffed white sofa (the Divorce Sofa, as I like to call it – both of my husbands hated white). Looking out at the city skyline, I remind myself again of how grateful I am to be here, in this city, this home, and living this life I rebuilt from the ground up.

After that Christmas night at the end of 2020, I had the clarity I needed. Leo and I met a few days later on a beach, sitting on a log with coffee, watching the waves break in big, frothy explosions onto the rocks.

EPILOGUE

"I'm ready to move on," I said quietly. As much as I knew it was the right decision for me, it still hurt. Endings are hard, but we can't have beginnings without them.

"Okay, I understand," he replied. He wrapped his arms around me and held me tight, and we cried together.

"I'm so grateful for you," I said. " I've grown more in our time together than ever before."

He held me tighter. "I feel the same way. We've had an incredible life together, and you've helped me grow in ways I never could have on my own."

We sat for a while longer in silence until the rain came down in a soft mist like a baptism. Then we walked back to the road.

"I'm this way," I said, pointing down the street.

"I know," he smiled. "Talk soon?"

I looked into his eyes, crinkled in a sad smile; the same eyes that had met mine in the Campidoglio in Rome, as we vowed to spend the rest of our lives together. The eyes that wouldn't meet mine during weeks of silent treatment. The eyes that flashed when he expressed anger or contempt.

"You bet," I said, then turned and walked home without looking back.

Once I'd finally said the words, I felt so much relief. I began to feel excited about my future and scared as hell, too. There's that *terrixcited* feeling again.

Divorce isn't a failure. Not when you know you deserve better. Then it's a success. It means that you know your time together is complete, you acknowledge that not every relationship is meant to last forever, and you're willing to say the scary things out loud.

I felt a surge of energy cascade into my life after that day. All that energy I'd spent on our relationship; trying to make it work, going to therapy, denying there were

Epilogue

problems, agonizing over the decision to stay or go – it all poured back into me.

All the work I'd done in my Selfish Year became the foundation for my reinvention.

The months I'd spent in solitude, going deep into myself, healing and finding my answers, became the catalyst for everything that came after.

I always tell my clients that change happens when you change yourself first. It seems easier to try and change our circumstances, or change our bodies, or change someone else, but it isn't because it doesn't last. It's like sticking a Band-Aid on an infected wound and hoping it will heal without ever treating the infection itself.

But when you commit to changing yourself first – creating safety for your First Girl, letting your Hurt Girl finally rest, and connecting to your Inner Being – when you commit to being selfish and making how you feel your priority – when you get obsessed with building a safe haven within – that's when everything changes in your life.

I decided to move to Vancouver for a fresh start. After raising kids in the suburbs for 20 years, I wanted to try the urban lifestyle. I this condo and moved within two weeks.

Soon after moving in, I felt excitement about taking better care of my body. I started drinking a gallon of water a day, cut out alcohol, and ate more vegetables and fruit.

I continued walking daily. Walking saved my life in so many ways. The ritual of getting outside and being in nature became something I craved, and living in Vancouver was perfect; I lived two blocks from the beach and three blocks from Stanley Park. I began wandering the forests of the park, gazing up at the huge old-growth trees, placing my hands on their ancient trunks, and listening to their wisdom.

206 EPILOGUE

In six months I lost 55 pounds and felt sexier, happier, and more alive than ever. I cut my hair short, and people from my past no longer recognized me, partly because of the physical transformation but mainly because I glowed from the inside out. When I look at pictures from just a few years ago, I see a woman who's smiling (because good girls smile for the camera), but my eyes are dead. Now I smile with my whole being, and guess what? I have dimples in my cheeks that I never knew existed!

I started sharing my story of the Selfish Year with my online communities. It was scary initially because I never wanted my message to be about me. What I realized, however, is that when I shared my story, thousands of women would comment, telling me how much it helped them. It showed them that they're not crazy, they're not alone, and they don't have to hide.

I began talking more about my experiences, which led me to start *The Selfish Woman* podcast. Now I get to speak with incredible women who also know the value of being selfish and share their stories of transformation.

As I'm writing this, I look around at my beautiful home and everything I've created. Pictures of me and the kids hang on the walls, memories from a family trip. Candles flicker on the coffee table, bouncing light off the crystals I've collected over the past couple of years. I've made an incredible life for myself and I did it all on my own. I've done a solo trip to Joshua Tree and even went back to Italy one summer. We had some unfinished business, Italy and me.

The day I got my divorce papers from my lawyer, I filmed myself opening the envelope and reading the documents because I wanted to show that divorce doesn't have to be a devastating failure. It can also be a powerful opportunity for reinvention. When I read the words "Your divorce has been finalized," I felt such a mix of emotions: sadness, grief, and heartache. I missed Leo so much. He'd been my best friend for years, which was a real loss for me. I also felt relief, pride, and excitement. I'd closed this chapter of my life. I did it all on my own. I didn't wait for someone else to choose for me, and I didn't rely on someone else to tell me what to do. I worked my ass off, figured out how to trust myself and make decisions on my own, and learned how to stay true to those, even when it was hard, even when it disappointed someone else.

I've talked about my doubts regarding the Selfish Experiment and how I wondered if it was legitimate, or simply a privileged experience. I have questioned whether I could have done this when I was a stay-at-home mother of three with no job and financially dependent on my husband.

What I see now, and what I want you to know, is that being selfish is not a privileged practice. Yes, I had an entire year to dedicate to my growth and healing, and I'm incredibly grateful for that experience. It allowed me to fast-track my experience, to take all those lessons and pass them on to you.

You can be a Selfish Woman right where you are, at whatever stage of your life, and whatever you're experiencing. Whether you're a young woman just starting out, a mom of young kids or teenagers, transitioning to an empty nester, or child-free, you can be a Selfish Woman.

Whether you're single, married, separated, divorced, or anything in between, you can be a Selfish Woman.

Whether you have a career or job or are a stay-at-home mom, you can be a Selfish Woman.

Being a Selfish Woman has nothing to do with your circumstances and everything to do with your perspective.

Take the Selfish Strategies and use them daily, even if it's five minutes in the morning or a few minutes at the end of the day in the bathtub (or sitting on the floor of your bathroom with the door locked).

208 EPILOGUE

Take a bit of time every day to remind yourself that you matter, that you are the most important person in your life, and that you deserve to be a priority.

Remember that when you are selfish, you fill your cup first. Then you can give to others from overflow, abundance and joy, instead of exhaustion, resentment and burnout.

Remember that even small daily actions will move you toward the life you deserve.

I lived most of my life trying to be selfless, good, polite, and sweet, and it got me nowhere but miserable, resentful, overwhelmed, exhausted, and unhealthy.

Now I know the truth: When women throw off the conditioning of the patriarchy, when we let go of the old beliefs that kept us chained, when we see the cage we've been put in and set ourselves free, we become unstoppable. No one is coming to save you; no one will do it for you. You must set yourself free.

And how you set yourself free is to become a Selfish Woman.

And in becoming a Selfish Woman, not only will you set yourself free, but you will free future generations. You will become a role model for others to see what it looks like to be a powerful, independent, and confident woman.

It's time for you to take radical responsibility for your life, do the work to heal and grow every day, and create a life that is a reflection of the magic that exists within you.

You are magical. You are magnificent. You are fabulous.

Start living like it's true, and one day you'll turn around and be amazed at what you see. You'll see a woman who loves herself beyond measure, loves her people fiercely, and does whatever the fuck she wants.

Resources

I have several programs that can be the next step in your journey to becoming a Selfish Woman.

Women Rising is a 12-module course with accompanying workbooks. It is designed to guide you through emotional healing, rewiring your mind to accept change, working through fear, loving your body, and creating a personalized spiritual practice. Bonuses include Get Off the Fence and a one-year membership to The Phoenix, my group coaching program.

Get Off the Fence is a six-module course with accompanying workbooks. This program guides you through everything you need to consider and work through, to make the decision to stay or leave your relationship.

The Phoenix is my group coaching program designed to support you to rise from the ashes of the past and soar into a new, powerful future. We meet twice every month on Zoom where I teach and do hot-seat coaching. You also get access to a private community for sisterhood and support.

Unapologetic AF is a five-module course that guides you through everything you need to know to become a badass at boundaries.

All these programs and more can be found at www .valeriejonescoach.com/courses. If you're interested in working with me as a private client, apply here: www .valeriejonescoach.com/services.

The Selfish Woman podcast is available on Apple podcasts, Spotify, and many other podcast providers.

Social Media: I am @thevaleriejones on Instagram, and @valeriejones11 on TikTok

Acknowledgments

This book represents the dreams of my First Girl, who used to write stories about magic and mystery in her room at night.

It also would never have happened without the collective wisdom, guidance, influence, and support of countless people, some of whom I want to acknowledge here.

To my brilliant agent, Jen, for believing in this book and finding it a home, and for reminding me that "you only need one." To Jennie for bringing us together.

To the team at Jossey Bass, you truly are a dream team, and I'm so lucky I get to partner with you. Your support and belief in this book have changed my life—especially Amy, Sophie, Adaobi, and Moses.

For my friends who have cheered me on, reminded me that I'm enough, and kicked my ass when I needed it.

ACKNOWLEDGMENTS

To Shari for reading my first draft and telling me the truth. You were the safe space for me to start thinking I might be on to something.

To all my clients, past, present, and future, who come to my retreats, take my courses, and sit across from me with your vulnerability, your pain, and your dreams. I'm honored to partner with you in your transformation. You are all my heroes.

To my children, everything I do is for you. I love you more than you'll ever know, and I'm constantly inspired by you.

About the Author

Valerie Jones is the host of the popular podcast *The Selfish Woman*, and founder of the Selfish Woman Movement. Her international reach is delivered through courses, retreats, and the advice she shares on her social media platforms. Her expertise has developed from over a decade of working with clients as a Certified Coach, and she is leading a movement of women who are done playing small and are ready to choose themselves—without guilt, without apology, and without looking back.

With her no-BS approach to personal transformation, Valerie has guided thousands of women to reclaim their power, rewrite their stories, and design lives that feel as good as they look.

Based in Vancouver, British Columbia, Valerie is mom to three amazing and now grown-up kids and is currently enjoying her empty next with a big white couch and a view of the city. She spends her days walking along the Pacific

ABOUT THE AUTHOR

Ocean and wandering through Stanley Park, having deep conversations with trees (they make great listeners).

When she's not coaching, writing, or making her next TikTok, you'll find her planning her next solo adventure, roaming the city, or diving into soul-shaking conversations about life, love, and reinvention.